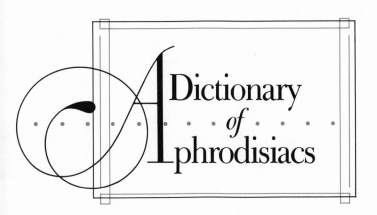

A Dictionary
of
Aphrodisiacs

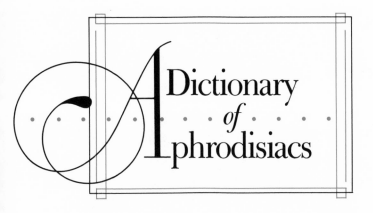

by
Harry E. Wedeck

Illustrated by
Jill Karla Schwarz

Designed by
Joyce Rothschild

A Pomegranate Production

Philosophical Library Inc.
New York

ISBN-0-8022-2562-4
Published 1989 by Philosophical Library.
Co-edited by Jenna Bassin and Jane Lahr.
Copyright 1989 by Allied Books, Inc., New York, N.Y.
Manufactured in the United States of America.

I will show you a philtre without potions, without herbs, without any witch's incantation: if you wish to be loved, love.

Seneca

ABSINTHE

A liqueur made in France from Artemisia absinthium, a plant native to North Africa and the foothills and valleys of European mountain ranges. The liqueur is green in color and is compounded of marjoram, oil of aniseed, dill, and other aromatic oils.

Artemisia absinthium, also known as wormwood, was used in ancient times to banish demons. It was associated with the rites of St. John's Eve, when a crown of the plant was supposed to ward off evil spirits. Tradition has it that John the Baptist wore a girdle of wormwood while he was in the wilderness.

Wormwood was dedicated to the Greek goddess Artemis, hence the name Artemisia absinthium. Other classical references to this herb are Dioscorides, a Greek physician of the first century A.D., who declared that it prevented intoxication. The Roman scholar Pliny the Elder endorsed it as a great sexual restorative.

· · · · · · · 7 · · · · · · ·

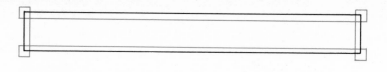

Absinthe was used extensively as a sexual stimulant by turning-of-the century artistic communities, especially in Paris. It is considered to be dangerous taken in large quantities.

In England the plant is called Green Ginger and Old Woman. Other names for the plant are Boy's Love, Lad's Love, and Maiden's Ruin.

AGATE

Like a great many other stones, precious and semi-precious, the agate has a reputation for stimulating amorous activity.

AISCHROLOGIA

The frank expression of obsenities is considered to be an indirect sexual stimulant and was common in ancient Greek comedy, particularly that of Aristophanes. Famous literary examples of the twentieth century are James Joyce's *Ulysses*, D.H. Lawrence's *Lady Chatterly's Lover* and the books of Henry Miller.

ALBERTUS MAGNUS

This great medieval theologian and scientist, who was the teacher of Thomas Aquinas, offered numerous formulas for love potions in his works. He particularly recommends the brains of a partridge calcined into a powder and swallowed in red wine.

ALCHEMICAL APHRODISIAC

In the Middle Ages the alchemists sold a putative aphrodisiac which included gold as an ingredient. The

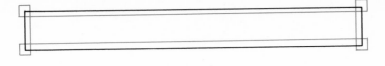

preparation was in the form of a beverage to be taken daily and was called "potable gold."

ALCOHOL

Alcohol with sugar added was used to promote the amorous feelings of King Louis XIV. In some European countries it was a folk custom to offer a bride and bridegroom cakes moistened with sugar and alcohol.

In small amounts, alcohol removes inhibitions by depressing the "higher centers" of the brain and often is the major ingredient in aphrodisiacs. Sexual desire may be increased; however, consummation is negligible or abortive. As the Porter in Shakespeare's *Macbeth* put it, "It (alcohol) provokes the desire, but it takes away the performance."

ALMONDS

The Perfumed Garden, an erotic handbook written by a sixteenth century Arab sheik, recommends almonds as an aphrodisiac: "Drink a glassful of very thick honey, eat twenty almonds and one hundred grains of the pine tree before bedtime. Continue for three successive days."

ALMOND NECTAR

4 servings

1 cup milk	1/8 tsp. cinnamon
6 raw almonds	1/8 cup dates

Mix together in a blender and serve hot or cold.

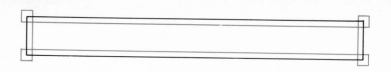

ALMOND SOUP

This aphrodisical soup contains powdered almonds, yolk of eggs, chicken stock, and cream. Many so-called aphrodisiac recipes are basically wholesome ingredients prepared in a tasty way. The receptivity to romance probably comes from the general sense of relaxation and well-being good food induces.

AMAZONS

According to Eustathius, the twelfth century historian and scholar, the ancient Amazons had the strange custom of breaking the leg or arm of any captive taken in battle. The intention was not to prevent the possibility of escape, but to render the captive more vigorous for amatory conflicts, as the Amazons imagined that the genital members would be strengthened by the deprivation of one of the captive's limbs. Hence, when reproached by the Scythians for the limping gait of her slaves, Queen Antianara replied, "The lame best perform the act of love."

AMBER

In old pharmacopoeias many formulas were enumerated in which amber constituted the base. These recipes were all directed toward amatory capacity as their names imply, e.g.: Tables of Magnanimity, Electuary Satyrion, Joy Powder.

AMBERGRIS

A waxy substance found in tropical seas, believed to be the secretion in the intestines of the sperm whale. Used in cooking as an aphrodisiac.

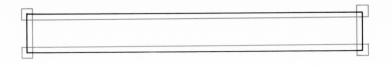

Among the Persians, pastilles consisting of powdered ambergris, rubies, gold, and pearls were eaten as an aphrodisiac.

In the Orient, ambergris is still considered a potent aphrodisiac. Coffee is often served with a little ambergris at the bottom of the cup. According to one authority, three grains of ambergris are sufficient to produce, among other effects, a disposition to cheerfulness and sexual desire.

Among the ancients, ambergris was also used to restore vital powers that had been exhausted by old age or excess.

AMOROUS INDUCEMENT

In giving advice on love and sex to his fellow Romans, the poet Ovid emphasizes a number of points that favor erotic conditions: a suntan, cleanliness, neat dress, brushed teeth, well-fitting sandals, and a good haircut.

For women Ovid suggests an elegant coiffure, dress that is becoming to the wearer's shape and complexion, a graceful gait, well-controlled laughter when the occasion arises. For erotic interaction Ovid advises aggressivess. "Love hates laziness," he warns.

ANANGA-RANGA

A Sanskrit manual written by Kalyanamalla, similar in content to Ovid's *Ars Amatoria*. This guide has been translated into a number of Indian languages, and also was translated into English by Sir Richard

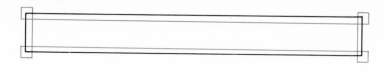

Burton. It deals with a vast array of love-making techniques, cosmetic and beautifying hints, aphrodisiac prescriptions, magic onintments for securing and retaining affection and love for both men and women, perfumes, bodily hygiene, hair treatments, drugs, philtres, pills, incense, charms for erotic subjugation, and magic incantations for the purpose of fascination.

ANAPHRODISIACS

Excessive indulgence in alcohol diminishes sexual desire. Hindu texts often mention this condition. It is also familiar to the ancient classical writers. Tobacco and the plant valerian are also considered to be anaphrodisiac in their effects.

Water-purslan, cucumbers, even a drink of water have all had a reputation as being antiaphrodisiacs. Other means of cutting down sexual desire are a spare diet, a laborious life, little sleep, and much bodily exercise.

In ancient times, a cool regimen was suggested for quenching desire. Plato and Aristotle advised going barefoot as a means of checking the stimulus to carnal pleasure. The cold bath was considered equally efficacious. Others, including Pliny the Elder who authored the *Historia Naturalis*, and the physician Galen, the second century A.D. Greek authority whose reputation extended far into the Middle Ages, advised thin sheets of lead to be worn on the calves of the legs and near the kidneys.

In his *Remedia Amoris*, the Roman poet Ovid had the

following to say about subduing sexual energy:

> *Venus loves idleness. If you seek an*
> *end to love, be active, you will be*
> *safe.... Take up law...or busy yourself*
> *with agriculture...or hunting...or*
> *fishing...magic rites are useless. Think*
> *of our love's faults and defects, avoid*
> *solitude. Shun loving couples, shun*
> *public groups, public performances,*
> *and shows. And avoid certain aphro-*
> *disiac foods, such as onions and*
> *rockets (a form of cabbage).*

In a general sense, intense mental study, neurotic anxiety, fasting, excessive sleep, snuff-taking, have all been at various times considered detrimental to amatory activity.

ANCHOVIES

In Southern European countries, they have long been reputed to be lust-provoking. If nothing more, they are gastronomically appealing.

ANGEL WATER

First used by the Portuguese. Popular in the eighteenth century. Shake together a pint of orange flower water, a pint of rose water, a half pint of myrtle water. Add two thirds of distilled spirit of musk, two thirds of spirit of ambergris. A reputed aphrodisiac aid.

ANISE

A plant indigenous to the Eastern Mediterranian area.

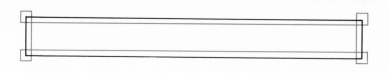

As a culinary ingredient it acts as a sexual stimulant and enjoys a reputation as such among gourmets.

ANTS

A medieval aphrodisiac recipe contained dried black ants. Oil was poured over them and they were enclosed in a glass jar, ready for use.

ANVALLI

A sexual stimulant mentioned in the Hindu erotic manual *Ananga-Ranga*. It consists of the outer shell of the anvalli nut, from which the juice is extracted. Dried in the sun, this juice is mixed with powder of the same nut. The compound is eaten with candied sugar, clarified butter, and honey.

APADRAVYAS

In Hindu erotology, these are objects of various kinds and designs, mostly metallic, that are used in connection with sexual activity. They are primarily intended to aid and prolong erection.

APHRODISIA

A popular Greek festival held in honor of the goddess Aphrodite, patroness of love. At this festival prostitutes and hetairai, the Greek name for courtesans, were important participants.

APHRODISIAC CAKES

In ancient Syracuse, cakes were made in the shape of the female genitalia and offered in divine sacrificial rites. Pastries resembling both male and female sex organs were common in medieval times, particularly

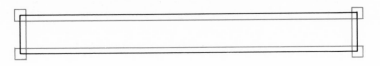

in Germany.

An English example was called "cockle bread." A young girl would knead a small piece of dough and then press it to her vulva. This mold was then baked and offered to the man of her choice. If the fellow ate it, he would fall under her spell.

Aphrodisiac Ointment

A recipe for an ointment to be applied to the male genitalia before sex consists of powdered white thorn-apple, king pepper, black pepper and honey. Aside from the lubricating powers of the honey, the pepper ingredients may actually aid erection by increasing the blood supply. Chemicals present in the thorn-apple are absorbed through the tissues of both male and female sex organs. These chemicals have properties that would induce, excitement, sedation and hallucination.

Aphrodisiac Pill

A Chinese pill intended to augment virile capacity. It is described by the Orientalist and anthropologist Sir Richard Burton as rhubarb colored, and enclosed in a wax capsule. The composition of the pill consists of vegetable extracts and vegetable matter. Dissolved in water, it is applied to the generative member.

Aphrodisiacs

By definition, aphrodisiacs imply a stimulus to love. The term is derived from Aphrodite, the Greek goddess, in her capacity as a personification of the sexual urge, generation, and the power of love. To the Greek and Roman poets, Aphrodite is the generative force that pervades the entire cosmos.

In his poem *De Rerum Natura* the Roman poet Lucretius invokes the goddess under her Roman name of Venus:

> *Mother of the descendants of Aeneas, delight*
> *of men and gods, O nourishing Venus,*
> *beneath the gliding constellations of heaven*
> *you fill the sea with sails and the lands with*
> *produce, since through you every kind of liv-*
> *ing creature is conceived, coming forth to*
> *gaze upon the light of the sun.*

Aphrodisiacs involve visual images, olfactory and tactile experiences, physiological operations related to food, drink, drugs, or conceptual pictures inducing libidinous thoughts and impulses. Some so-called aphrodisiacs are, though not effective, at least innocuous, while others may be extremely harmful and dangerous. It is wise, therefore, to take all aphrodisiacs, both figuratively and physiologically, with a grain of salt.

The usefulness of aphrodisiacs is often a matter of longstanding tradition, untested for validity, but wishfully handed down through the centuries in legends and folk tales, in magic rituals and old wives' lore. In most cases there has been no definitive pharmaceutical or medical approval to warrant such belief. What may be safely asserted is that an abundance of rich and appealing food, reinforced with palatable drinks, all consumed in a pleasant atmosphere in congenial company, will unquestionably induce a feeling of euphoria that may tend toward sensual directions.

For centuries writers have discussed the use of aphrodisiacs. Rabelais (1490-1553) wrote wittily and in detail on this subject in *Gargantua and Pantagruel* wherein he recommends a moderate intake of wine:

> *As is implied by the old proverb, which saith that Venus takes cold when not accompanied by Ceres and Bacchus.... The philosophers say that 'idleness is the mother of luxury.' Who were able to rid the world of loitering and laziness might easily frustrate and disappoint Cupid of all his designs, aims, engines, and devices, and so disable and appall him that his bow, quiver, and darts should from thenceforth be a mere needless load and burden to him, for that it could not then lie in his power to strike or wound any of either sex, with all the arms he had. He is not, I believe, so expert an archer, as that he can hit cranes flying in the air, or yet the young stags skipping through the thickets,...that is to say, people moiling, stirring, and hurrying up and down, restless, and without repose. He must have those hushed, still, quiet, lying at a stay, lither, and full of ease, whom he is able to pierce with all his arrows.*

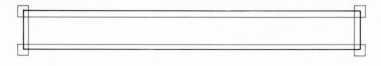

Diogenes defined lechery as the occupation of folks destitute of all other occupation. Seneca, the Roman philosopher and tutor of the Emperor Nero says that love is a mental condition fostered by leisure. Further,

> *Love is a mighty force of the mind, and a*
> *gentle mental heat produced by youthful lust,*
> *nourished by idleness amidst the good things*
> *that life brings.*

APHRODISIACS FOR SALE

In ancient Rome, love concoctions of all kinds were sold publicly. Poets and imperial officials, travelers and roués, idle matrons and hardened soldiers, resorted to such aphrodisiac support without hesitation of self-consciousness.

APHRODISIAC WINE

An Italian recipe that has a presumptive amatory effect contains wine, ginger, cinnamon, rhubarb, and vanilla.

APHRODITE

> *The great and amorous sky curved over the*
> *earth, and lay upon her as a pure lover.*
> *The rain, the humid flux descending from*
> *heaven for both man and animal, for both*
> *thick and strong, germinated the wheat,*
> *swelled the furrows with fecund mud,*
> *and brought forth the buds in the orchards.*
> *And it is I who empowered these moist*
> *espousals, I, the great Aphrodite....*
>
> Aeschylus, *The Danaides*

The great, the golden Aphrodite. What better appelation could there be for this powerful manifestation of the primordial feminine energy of the universe? Gold is the color of the heart chakra and it is the heart that unites what is below with what is above, the body with soul, the emotions with the intellect, the earth with the heavens. Aphrodite, Goddess of Love, is the essence of loving attachment and the source of the earth's fecundity. As Aphrodite Ourania she is Queen of Heaven, goddess of the purest love. As Aphrodite Pandemos, she is the principle of amity and loving kindness that civilizes the human race. Further association with this civilizing aspect are the Aphrodite influence through beauty of dress, and the beauty of the garden.

Aphrodite, the Foam-born. It is said that when she emerged from the sea that gave her life, the earth burst into flower wherever she stepped. Laughter and beauty, love and desire, fertility and abundance, are her gifts to us.

It is no wonder that those objects and substances believed to enhance the desire for union between woman and man, and the vigor to consummate it, to strengthen our ability to bear children, grow crops, and otherwise create our world, are called aphrodisiacs.

The dark side of Aphrodite is her aspect as the obsessive, possessive lover. This is reflected in some of the philtres and potions that were intended to subjugate

or enthrall the object of love whether they wished it or not.

The higher aspects of physical union are expressed in the erotic literature and practices of many cultures from antiquity to the present. Hindu, Arab, and Chinese love manuals all express respect and even reverence for the physical union of male and female which is seen as a reflection of higher, divine union. This stress on the importance of a properly balanced exchange of sexual energies goes back to our earliest beginnings and can be read in the rites accompanying the ancient rituals of the Fertile Crescent civilizations and those of proto-historical India.

APHRODITE KALLIPYGOS

Aphrodite, the Greek goddess of love, was represented, in poetry and sculpture, as endowed with such alluring charms, such sexual enticements, as to infatuate even the wise man, as Homer adds. Throughout Greece, in temples dedicated to the goddess, her kallipygian beauty was stressed as a factor in her worship. (see KALLIPYGIAN COQUETRY)

APOTHECARY BURTON

In the seventeenth century an English apothecary named Robert Burton opened a factory in the town of Colchester where he produced aphrodisiac confections derived from sea holly roots. Sea holly (or eryngo) which grows wild along the English coast is mentioned by a number of Elizabethan writers, including Dryden and Shakespeare, in connection with aphrodi-

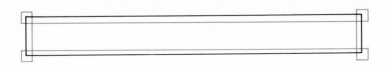

siacs. Burton's candies were called "kissing comfits." (see ERYNGO)

APPLE

In ancient Greece and in Rome the apple had a symbolic erotic connotation. Lovers or would-be lovers exchanged apples as presents, or threw them to each other.

Mythologically, a certain Acontius was in love with Cydippe. As the love was reciprocated, he wrote 'I swear by Artemis that I will wed Acontius on an apple. Cydippe read the words aloud, and although she threw the apple away, she finally accepted Acontius.

Powdered white thorn-apples, black pepper, honey, long pepper, compounded into an ointment, is recommended, in Hindu sexology, as an irresistable means of achieving sexual mastery. (see APHRODISIAC OINTMENT)

In medieval Germany it was a popular belief that an apple steeped in the perspiration of the loved woman would excite amorous advances.

Ancient Scandinavian legends describe apples as food of the gods. The belief was that the gods, grown old and decrepit, were rejuvenated by feasting on apples.

APRICOT BRANDY

Considered an aphrodisiac liqueur. The probable reason is that it is pleasant in itself and is conducive to a relaxed condition of well-being.

APULEIUS

A Roman orator and philosopher who flourished in the second century A.D. He also wrote a strange romantic novel entitled *The Golden Ass* or *Metamorphoses*. It contains exciting adventures, magic episodes, unique festivals and rites, and a great deal of matter relating to sexual activities, aphrodisiacs and erotic rituals.

The novel has the force of a verbal aphrodisiac. It belongs in the same a category as the *Decameron* and Honoré de Balzac's *Contes Drólatiques*.

AQUAMARINE

An engraved aquamarine was used among Arabs as a love charm to secure conjugal fidelity.

ARABIAN NIGHTS

In the story of Ala-al Din Abu-Al, a druggist prepares a love potion containing cubebs, a variety of pepper:

> *After hearing Sham-al Din's story, the druggist betook himself to a hashish seller, of whom he bought two ounces of concentrated Roumi opium and equal parts of Chinese cubebs, cinnamon, cloves, cardamom, ginger, white pepper, and mountain shiek—an aphrodisiac lizard; and pounding them all together boiled them in sweet olive oil; after which he added three ounces of male frankincense in fragments and a cupful of coriander*

*seed, and macerating the whole made it into
an electuary with Roumi bee-honey. Then he
put the confection in the bowl and carried it
to the merchants, saying:*

*Take of my electuary with a spoon after sup-
ping, and wash it down with a sherbet made
of rose conserve; but first sup off mutton and
house pigeon plentifully seasoned and hotly
spiced.*

ARABS

Of all peoples, the Arabs have made almost a science
or erotic writing. Their literature abounds in studies
and manuals that discuss the physiology of love,
amorous skills, aphrodisiacs and anaphrodisiacs, in a
wider sense, the entire range of sexual relationships.

The Perfumed Garden, one of the major erotic manuals originally intended for Moslem use, is full of anecdotes illustrating some particular phase of
lovemaking—pervaded, in most cases, by expressions
of devoutness, sanctity, poetic imagery, and verse.
Human sexuality was regarded as sacred and the
stimulation of desire was considered a devout duty.

ARMAGNAC

Henry VI of France, before confronting his numerous
mistresses, regularly fortified himself with a tiny glass
of this dry brandy named for the Armangnac region
of southwest France.

AROMATIC BATHS

Among the Romans, especially in the luxurious Impe-

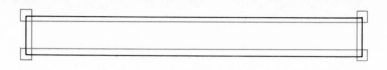

rial Age, aromatic baths constituted a regular prelude and instigation for erotic practice. Similarly, perfumed unguents were used by attendants who massaged the bodies of the bathers.

The impact of perfume on sexual response has long been known to Oriental sexologists: Arabic manuals are packed with hints and advice on the use of such aids. Contemporary scientists are discovering that the Arabs were right. (see PERFUME and PHERAMONES)

ARTEMISIA

This genus of aromatic plants includes wormwood and mugwort. Used as a condiment in erotic cookery.

ARTICHOKE

A bristly plant whose edible parts are the fleshy bases of the leaves. Considered a powerful aphrodisiac, especially in France. Street vendors in Paris had a special cry:

> *Artichokes! Artichokes!*
> *Heats the body and the spirit.*
> *Heats the genitals.*

Artichokes were popular as an aphrodisiac since they supposedly have the power to prevent premature ejaculation. (This is not proven.) However, eating artichokes may directly produce euphoria which, in an indirect fashion, is accompanied by the pleasant kind of relaxation conducive to lovemaking.

2 small to medium globe artichokes
1/2 cup diced onion
1 garlic clove crushed
1/2 cup diced celery
2 Tbsp. sunflower seeds

1 Tbsp. olive oil
1 1/4 cups cooked brown rice
1 tsp. dried mint
juice of 1/2 lemon
2 Tbsp. parsley
1/2 cup crummbled feta cheese

Remove the stems of the artichokes as well as the discolored, tough bottom row of leaves. Bring two inches of water to a boil. Place artichokes in a steamer and cover. Steam for about 35 minutes. They should be tender enough to pull the leaves out easily. Let cool at room temperature.

Stuffing
Sauté the sunflower seeds, celery, onion, garlic in the oil until the onions are clear. Then mix with rice, mint, lemon and parsley. Remove the top leaf cluster from the artichokes and scoop out the hairy center. Be careful not to remove the tender heart just below the hairy bit. Spread out the leaves and fill with the Passion Pilaf. Cover with feta cheese and bake at 325 degrees for 25 minutes. Place on small decorative plates and eat by candlelight.

ASOKA

In Hindu sexology the asoka plant, the lotus, and the jasmine stimulate desire. The lotus itself is associated with the Lotus-Woman, the Hindu feminine ideal.

ASPARAGUS

A daily dish of asparagus, first boiled then fried in fat, with egg yolks and a sprinkling of condiments, will,

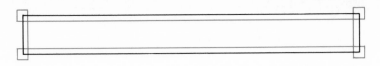

according to an Arab manual, produce considerable erotic effect.

ASS

In Greek mythology, the ass was the symbol of sexual potency. This animal was associated with satyrs and sileni, creatures who in their characteristics resembled satyrs.

On one occasion, at a Dionysiac festival, Priapus, personification of the sexual impulse, was about to consummate his sexual desire for the nymph Lotis. The braying of an ass, however, interrupted the performance. Since then, the ass became a sacrificial victim of Priapus.

AUDILE APHRODISIAC

The voice, in inflection or tone or volume or by some other peculiarity of the individual, can be a deeply stirring incitement. Thus it is possible to fall in love with a voice, both fictionally and in reality.

BACCHUS

Roman name for Dionysus, the ancient Greek divinity of wine and fertility whose cult was marked by orgiastic revelries. Festivals involved procreative rites and phallic worship. (see DIONYSUS)

BAH-NAMEH

Book of Delight. A Turkish collection of amorous tales by Abdul Hagg Effendi. Contains allusions to aphrodisiacs.

BAIAE

An ancient Roman pleasure resort, somewhat like contemporary Nice. It was the focal point of all kinds of erotic experiments, unbridled debauchery, amorous intrigues and excitations.

Seneca, the philosopher and tutor to the emperor Nero, inveighs against the abandoned and lascivious atmosphere of the resort. It is, he declares in one of his Letters, characterized by all-night revelry, drunkenness on the beach, banquets in boats, and uninhibited orgies and festivities. All this, apart from the hot sulphur springs that were the ostensible object of visitors who sought curative treatments, tended to extreme aphrodisiac diversions. (see SPA)

BAMBOO SHOOTS

They are believed to produce aphrodisiac reactions. Popular in the Orient, particularly in China, in culinary practice.

BANANAS

Considered to have stimulating aphrodisiac properties, probably because of their phallic shape.

BARBEL

This fish, well-prepared, helps to restore virility. The tradition is old but in line with the general view of the stimulating properties of fish. Barbel was favored by the Roman emperor Tiberius who constantly sought sexual rejuvenation and made extensive use of aphrodisiacs.

BASIL

An aromatic plant used in food as a condiment with a reputation for having aphrodisiac effects. According to an early nineteenth century physician, basil "helps the difficiency of Venus." In Italy, basil was used as a love charm by young girls.

BATH

In the luxurious and free-wheeling Roman Imperial Age, baths that both men and women used in common were in vogue. In addition to the special hot, cold, and steam rooms available for the pleasure of the patrons, the bath attendants were of opposite sexes. Consequently, attendants and bathers were exposed to each other's allure during the entire procedure.

In the Middle Ages it was customary for young women to serve in a similar capacity as attendants to cavaliers and knights during their bathing. This was true particularly in Germany, where the public baths became virtual brothels.

BEANS

St. Jerome forbade nuns to partake of beans because they are supposedly a strong stimulant of the genitals.

In ancient Greek comedy an elderly character consults an oracle for aid in his senescent condition. The oracle's reply involved a dish of lentils.

BEEFSTEAK

Havelock Ellis, the sexologist, regarded the beefsteak as "probably as powerful a sexual stimulant as any food."

BEER

In England, popular belief attributes to beer a coital stimulus. Medical authority recommends that beer be taken along with food. Like all alcohol intake related to sex, a little goes a long way and over-indulgence confounds the goal.

BEETS

White beets are mentioned by Pliny the Elder, the
Roman encyclopedist, as helpful in promoting amorous capacity. In general, beets, carrots, and turnips
are all considered to be of aphrodisiac virtue.

BHANG

A Sanskrit term meaning hemp. In India the leaves
and seeds of hemp are chewed as a means of increasing sexual capacity. Frequently the seeds of hemp are
mixed with musk, sugar and ambergris, to which aphrodisiac virtues are also ascribed. The seed capsules
and leaves are often used to make an infusion, which
is drunk as a liquor. Insofar as anything that lowers
inhibitions is an aphrodisiac, it is effective.

BHUYA-KOKALI

A Hindu plant, botanically termed Solanum Jacquini,
that is suggested by the Hindu *Ananga-Ranga*, the
erotic guide, as a factor in inducing aphrodisiac
power. The juice of the plant is dried in the sun and
then mixed with honey, clarified butter, and sugar.

BIRD NEST SOUP

An extremely aphrodisiac Chinese preparation. The
nests are those of the sea swallow, made from sea
weed that is edible. The leaves are stuck together by
fish spawn, which abounds in phosphorus. The soup,
in addition, is highly spiced. (see PHOSPHORUS)

BIRTHWORT

A shrub in use among the Romans as an aphrodisiac,

also used in medieval times.

BITTERSWEET

An herb that was reputed to have aphrodisiac value. However, this is probably a tradition and untested.

BOCCACCIO (GIOVANNI) ON LOVE

Beauty is a fatal gift for those who want to live virtuously.

In love, however, women are brave. How many clamber over rooftops of houses and palaces, when their lovers await them! How many hide their admirers in chests or closets, before their husbands' very eyes! How many, lying next to him, have had them come even into their beds!

If you pursue the study of beautiful women they will teach you that those who play with love trifle away their chance to become happy through it.

BONE

A Hindu erotic text suggests the stimulating and alluring effect of bone of peacock or hyena, covered with gold and tied to the right hand.

BOOK OF AGE—REJUVENATION IN THE POWER OF CONCUPISCENCE

An Arab amatory manual by Ahmad bin Sulayman. Deals with many phases of sexology, and makes specific recommendations along erotic lines.

BOOK OF EXPOSITION

This is an Arabic erotic work entitled Kitab al-Izah fi'llm al-Nikah b-it-w-al-Kamal. Attributed, but not definitively, to a certain Jalai ad-din as-Siyuti.

Although it deals in abundant and frank detail with the most intimate erotic procedures, its tone, like that of similar Oriental manuals, is free from contrived obscenity or ribaldry. There is, in fact, implicit throughout, an attitude of reverence for the universal cosmic force that divinely governs all such human conditions.

BORAX

According to seventeenth century belief, refined borax excites powerful desire. Nicolas Venette, a Frenchman, recommends it as a substance that readily pervades all parts of the body. It should, however, be used in moderation.

BOURBONS

The French dynasty of the Bourbons, whose ascendency began with Henry IV early in the seventeenth century and spread over France, Spain, and Sicily, were notorious for their amatory skills and their ingenuities in erotic foods and drinks.

BRAIN

The brain of calf, sheep, and pig, young and served fresh, is reputedly erotic in its effect. As a side dish in Mediterranean countries, brains are a special delicacy when properly prepared.

BRETON CUSTOM

Aphrodisiac techniques intended to cure sterility have been known to women for millennia. In one Breton town, a phallic statue was the focal point of such efforts. Taking some of the dust around the effigy, they swallowed it in the hope of receiving a beneficent response to their prayers for fertility.

BUTTERMILK BATH

A Hindu love manual suggests that women bathe in the buttermilk of a she-buffalo to discourage unwanted admirers. This anti-aphrodisiac is to be mixed with goplike powder, banupadika plant and yellow amarinth.

BROAD BEAN SOUP

In Italy, often taken as an assumed aphrodisiac. Beans in general have long been believed to possess amatory virtue.

BROTHELS

In the eighteenth century, in England, on account of the spreading knowledge that food and drink exerted definite influence on amatory expression, public brothels were at the same time eating houses.

BURGUNDY

Considered a wholesome aphrodisiac in moderation.

This is in line with traditional belief in the amatory encouragements produced by wines and liqueurs taken in moderation.

CABBAGE

Wild cabbage was a frequent ingredient in aphrodisiac preparations. This tradition goes back many centuries.

CAKES

In the Middle Ages, spiced cakes were often baked in a small oven, over the naked body of a woman who wanted to retain the affections of her lover. The witch who carried out the baking technique used this form of sympathetic magic to arouse desire in correspondence with the flaming heat of the oven.

The baked concoction would ultimately be offered to the object of the woman's love. Such cakes were sometimes consumed by both parties, the man and the woman, as a means of strengthening and binding passion.

The practice was common throughout Europe, and not unknown in other countries as well.

CAMEL BONE

As an aphrodisiac aid, Indian erotology suggests camel bone, dipped in the juice of the eclipta prostat plant, then burnt. The black pigment produced from the ashes is placed in a box also made of camel bone and then applied with antimony to the eyelashes with the pencil of a camel bone. The effect, it is hinted, will be erotic subjugation.

CAMEL'S FAT

Fat, melted down from the hump of the camel, is suggested in an Oriental manual as an aphrodisiac aid.

CAMEL'S MILK

When mixed with honey and taken for successive days, this drink produces marked potency, according to Arab tradition.

CAMPHOR

A form of camphor known as monobromated camphor is said to have an aphrodisiac effect. In the seventeenth century monks were compelled to smell and chew camphor to extinguish sexual desire.

Modern authorities, however, deny this property of camphor, although it has been used to counteract the conditions arising from nymphomania.

CAPERBERRY

The berry of the caper plant was considered a strong aphrodisiac. In the Bible, the term is used synonymously with sexual desire, "and the caperberry shall fail." *Ecclesiastes* 12.5.

CARAWAY

Caraway has a reputed aphrodisiac virtue. It is frequently mentioned in Oriental love manuals.

CARDAMOM

A pounded mixture of cardamom seeds, ginger, and cinnamon sprinkled over boiled onions and green peas is considered by Arabs a good dish for promoting sexual vigor.

CARDOON

A prickly plant, akin to the artichoke. The fleshy parts of the inner leaves are eaten as an aphrodisiac, especially in France.

CARMINA PRIAPEA

A collection of Latin poems, obscene and erotic, that hymn the potency of Priapus. See PRIAPUS

CARROTS

Among Arabs, carrots are eaten as an aphrodisiac. Stewed in milk sauce, they are recommended as helpful in sexual activity. In Greece the carrot was popular as a sexual medicine; it was called a *philtron*.

CASTOR OIL

Once popular among American Indians for erotic purposes.

CATANCY

A plant that the witches of ancient Thessaly, in Greece, used in love philtres.

CAVIAR

Caviar is generally considered to be a stimulant to sensual inclinations. It is invariably present at dinners and banquets that stress rich, exotic dishes accompanied by appropriate wines, and resulting, for the diners, in a sense of complete euphoria. Such a condition is highly conducive to erotic activity as French and other European fiction illustrates so lavishly.

CELERY

In eighteenth century France, celery soup was a means of whetting the appetite for love. Celery is often included in aphrodisiac recipes.

CELERY CREAM

This concoction is said to stimulate urgency of sexual desire.

CESTUS

The girdle of Venus, that had the power of exciting love.

In Homer's *Iliad*, this girdle is "the charm of love and desire, that subdues all the hearts of the immortal gods and mortal men."

CHAMPAGNE

Long associated in fiction as well as fact with erotic stimulation, intimate dining and sexual encounters. In general, wine has traditionally been viewed as a significant stimulus to amatory ventures.

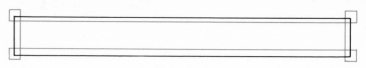

CHARMS

Among primitive and Oriental races love charms were often associated with the techniques known as *sympathetic magic*. A charm was uttered over betel nuts, the nuts were then placed in a box, and the person who opened the box fell passionately in love with the owner.

Another charm was uttered over the oil used by a woman, or over a lock of her hair. The hoped-for result was similar to an aphrodisiac stimulant.

CHEESE

Highly esteemed for its aphrodisiac propensities. In eighteenth century France, Parmesan cheese in particular was considered highly beneficial in this sense.

CHERRIES

Stimulating in an amatory sense, often included in love cookery.

CHESTNUTS

This compound was popular as an old English love recipe. Chestnuts, soaked in muscatel, then boiled, along with satyrion, pistachio nuts, pine kernels, cubebs, cinnamon, rocket seed and sugar.

CHICK-PEAS

Heat the juice of powdered onions and purified honey until the onion juice disappears. Cool the residue, then mix with water and pounded chick-peas. Taken before bedtime in winter, this beverage is described in an Arab manual as particularly stimulating.

CHINESE FOOD

Chinese have an intense fondness for the following foods, all of which, it is asserted, contribute to sexual potency when such foods are taken, not intermittently, but as a regular routine over an extended period of time: chicken liver, chicken gizzard, tripe, dried shrimp, celery, bamboo shoots, mushrooms, crab, melons, scallops, fried spinach, lettuce, noodles, shark fin, lobsters.

CHIN P'ING MEI

A Chinese picaresque erotic novel, written during the sixteenth century. Translated as *The Golden Lotus* by C. Egerton, also translated by Arthur Waley.

This long adventurous novel, somewhat in the manner of the *Metamorphoses*, is pervaded by amorous encounters, scenes in bordellos, feasts of lanterns, astrological lore, spells and aphrodisiac material, bawdry and cuckoldry, erotic techniques and sexual stimuli including the Monk's Pill, ointments, instruments, silver clasp and sulphur ring, a white silk ribbon with medicinal properties to increase desire, as well as constant references to the power of perfumes.

CHOCOLATE

In eighteenth century France, many aphrodisiac dishes and pastries were compounded with chocolate.

Cocoa, on the other hand, has been held to be anti-aphrodisiac.

Yet the belief in the aphrodisiac value of chocolate

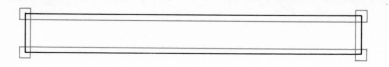

prevailed for a long time. In the seventeenth century, monks in France were forbidden to drink chocolate on account of its reputed amatory properties.

By the eighteenth century chocolate ceased to become a rarity. This loss of mystery probably accounts for its decline in popularity as an aphrodisiac. However, modern science has discovered that chocolate possesses a pleasure-producing chemical called phenylethylamine, the very same substance released by the brain when we fall in love.

CHUTNEY

A relish compounded of herbs, fruits and various seasonings. Commonly in use in the Orient, it has a reputation for stimulating the libido.

CINCIA

Also called Cinxia. A Roman goddess to whom the girdle of the bride was consecrated, symbolic of sexual surrender.

CINNAMON

The dried inner bark of an East India tree, used as a spice with reputed erotic effects. This cinnamon "cocktail" has been given credit for inducing lively desire: Crush one ounce each of cinnamon, vanilla bean, dried rhubarb and ginseng. Add these to two pints of chablis and let stand for two weeks. Be sure to stir daily. Strain through cheesecloth. Amber may be added for color.

Cinnamon Liqueur

Centuries ago, this drink was famous as an aphrodisiac but has gone out of use.

Civet

A perfume derived from the civet-cat. The French royal court used to offer sweets, perfumed with civet, to desirable ladies.

Civet-cats were bred for their secretions that formed the base of perfumes and were also of aphrodisiac value.

It is of interest to note that Daniel Defoe, author of *Robinson Crusoe*, was for a time the owner of a civet-cat farm.

Clams

Reputed to possess marked aphrodisiac virtue. Most kinds of sea-food have been credited with this property.

Cleopatra

Infamous Queen of Egypt in the first century B.C., renowned for her beauty and powers of seduction. She was mistress to Julius Caesar and Marc Antony. Legends say that she was accustomed to dissolve pearls in vinegar and drink the fluid in order to provoke her amorousness. Precious stones were always associated with magic properties, sometimes apocryphal, to ward off various evils and misfortunes that constantly beset mankind, and, on occasion, aphrodisiac in intent. Pearls were traditionally endowed with aphrodisiac virtue.

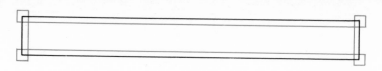

CLOTHING

In ancient Sparta, young women wore tunics ending above the knee and slit high at the side. For this reason the young women were known as "thigh-showers." The women of Sparta had a reputation for looseness and an aggressive sexuality.

COCAINE

This derivative of the coca plant has a reputation for aphrodisiac effect. However, to date there have been no studies on the specific results of cocaine use. It was recommended for the purpose of general stimulation and the heightening of sexual performance by none other than Sigmund Freud, who was subsequently pilloried for his views when the dangers of cocaine addiction became known.

In the early 20th century, many so-called tonics included cocaine as an ingredient. Originally Coca-Cola contained cocaine but its use was long ago discontinued and caffeine substituted as a stimulant.

To the extent that the drug induces feelings of euphoria, an increased sense of physical strength and the breakdown of inhibition, it can be said to stimulate erotic activity, particularly in men. However, prolonged use includes loss of sexual appetite among its side effects.

COD LIVER

Reputed to be a marked amatory stimulant. Most fish, in fact, are believed to have this virtue.

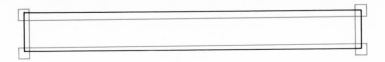

COD ROE

Considered to be a sexual stimulant and aid to fertility, as are the eggs of most other fish.

COFFEE

There is some controversy concerning coffee as an aphrodisiac. It has been believed that it dulls the sexual urge. A seventeenth century traveler to Persia describes the Khan drinking a black liquid called "kahowa"—coffee—as a deterrent to lasciviousness. However, certain alkaloids present in coffee help retain erection and delay orgasm.

COITUS

Speaking of the customs prevalent in India in connection with erotic practices, Nefzawi, author of *The Perfumed Garden*, enumerates twenty-nine postures of intimacy, a number of which are recommended only for yoga adepts. (see PERFUMED GARDEN)

COLA

An extensively used refreshing drink. It is also known as "bichy." It is obtained from the dried seeds of a plant called cola nitida. The seeds or nuts are common in Africa, where they are used as currency and often as charms and sacred objects.

Chewing cola is believed to endow a person with great vigor and is reputedly a sexual stimulant. It is a substance with a high caffeine content and is used in connection with celebrations and rituals.

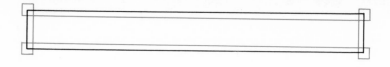

COLLYRIUM

A Latin term meaning *eye-salve*. Such salves, used by the Romans and the Hindus, were believed to have stimulating value in sexual relationships.

CONCUBINE

Among the Romans, sexual diversions, in the form of concubinage, were not frowned upon socially or publicly. Even on epitaphs women are described, without contempt, as having been concubines.

CORDAX

A provocative ancient Greek dance performed in honor of a Greek divinity named Artemis Cordakis. The dance consisted of sexual exhibitionism, reeling and swaying as if in a state of intoxication, erotic body movements and the unveiling of the nude body.

CORIANDER

An aromatic seed of a plant belonging to the carrot family. Albertus Magnus, the thirteenth century philosopher and occultist, states that coriander, valerian, and violet are love-producing herbs. They must, however, be gathered in the last quarter of the moon. Worn as a perfume, coriander oil promotes harmony in relationships.

CORINTH

In ancient times, this Greek port was notorious for its vast, ingenious, and expensive licentiousness. Horace, the Roman poet, makes this admission: "It is not everyone who can (afford to) go to Corinth."

In addition to the swarms of prostitutes and hetairae, there were numberless brothels and a temple dedicated to Aphrodite with a thousand attendants to celebrate her mysteries.

COUNTERCHARMS

When anaphrodisiac enchantments were effected on a victim, there was some redress at hand. Countercharms could be used. One such prescribes a virgin parchment, on which, before sunrise, and for nine successive days, the word *Arigazartor* was to be inscribed.

Another charm recommended: Pronounce the word TEMON three times at sunrise, on a day that gives promise of heralding fine weather.

COURTESANS

The courtesan in ancient times was such a normal social feature of life that among the Greeks and the Romans there are at least fifty terms to describe a courtesan, according to social status, location, appearance, and so on. In connection with this situation, there were state taxes, tax collectors, and city supervision. Far better educated in politics and the arts than their more respectable sisters, ancient courtesans achieved wealth, status, power, and fame as the gifted consorts of political and military leaders. One such was Aspasia, the mistress of Pericles of Athens.

COW WHEAT

Melampryum Pratense. A tall plant, with yellowish flowers. Used as food for cows. But Pliny the Elder, the Roman encyclopedist, and Dioscordies the physician say that it inflames the amatory passions.

CRAB APPLES

Often made into jellies and preserves and so reputed to have a stimulating effect.

CRAYFISH

Particularly in the Mediterranean littoral crayfish are considered of high aphrodisiac potency. Boiled in oil, with pepper, salt, garlic, and other spices, crayfish will reputedly provoke sexual excitation.

CRESS

A solitary plant, growing among ruins, old walls, in the fields. Used for salads, and as an aphrodisiac eaten raw, or boiled, or drunk as a juice. The plant is cultivated in the East for its sexual value.

Ovid, Martial, and Columella, all Roman poets, testify to its erotic power. Hence it was called *impudica,* shameless. Marcellus Empiricus, a Roman physician, prescribed three scruples of cress, three of red onion, three of pine seed, three of Indian nard, to cure impotence.

Apicius, author of a Roman cookbook, recommends, for the consummation of desire, onions cooked in water, with pine seeds or cress juice and pepper.

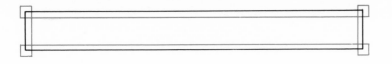

CRETE

On the island of Crete, in ancient times, a festival was held in honor of the god Hermes, at which all kinds of sexual indulgence were granted. The entire spectacle thus constituted a kind of general aphrodisiac stimulant.

CROCODILE

Crocodile teeth attached to the right arm will act as an aphrodisiac according to Pliny the Elder in his vast storehouse of ancient knowledge called *Historia Naturalis.*

The tail of a young crocodile is considered to be a sexual delicacy.

CUBEB

The cubeb, indigenous to Java, is a berry similar to a grain of pepper, with a pungent flavor. Used in cookery and medicine.

In China, an infusion of cubeb pepper leaves is prepared as a highly stimulating aphrodisiac.

Chewing cubeb pepper also produced similar results, so with powdered cubeb mixed with honey.

The eating of cubebs as a sexual inducement is suggested by the thirteenth century Arab philosopher and physician Avicenna.

CUCUMBER

Probably due to its phallic formation, the cucumber is often assumed to have aphrodisiac qualities.

CUMIN

An aromatic plant similar to fennel used as a condiment and credited as an erotic stimulus.

CURRY

An oriental dish flavored with spices. Reputedly a sexual stimulant. In a homeopathic view, any hot and spicy food will lead to a hot and spicy physical state.

CUTTLEFISH

The cuttlefish (or octopus), spiced oysters, sea hedgehogs, and lobsters were among the ingredients of love potions that the reputed magician Apuleius, who lived in the second century A.D., was accused of having prepared in order to win the love of a widow. There is a great deal of material on this subject in Apuleius' defense speech, *De Magia*, which is still in existence.

CYCLAMEN

The root of the flower cyclamen, or sowbread, was used in ancient times as an ingredient in love potions.

CAMIANA

Used in tantric sexual rites to prolong meditative states, this drug is obtained from the dried leaves of a plant called *turnera aphrodisiaca*. It is a shrub that grows in the lowlands of Brazil and is also found in Bolivia, Mexico and California. A powerful stimulant with aphrodisiac effects, it is toxic to the liver when used in excess.

DANCING

The ancient Romans frowned upon dancing, especially by women, as they considered it an erotic inducement. One Roman historian, Sallust, comments that a certain Sempronia danced more gracefully than a respectable woman should.

The Roman poet Ovid, author of the *Ars Amatoria*, recommends dancing to all girls who are in love.

At banquets and public performances of various kinds professional dancing-girls appeared. Generally, they were imported from Spain or Syria. Skilled in erotic movements and manipulations, they readily provoked the sensual desires of the spectators. The Roman satirist Juvenal describes them as writhing and wriggling frantically to the musical accompaniment of their own castanets, to excite sluggish lovers.

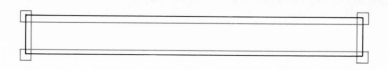

DATES

Preserved dates are believed by some gourmets to possess the power to stimulate erotic feelings.

DIASATYRION

Diasatyrion root taken morning and night with a little wine or cow's milk for an entire week will restore sexual vitality even in the elderly. The Persians called it "syrup of the fox."

DIET

The importance of a diet as a sexual factor is abundantly attested in the ancient writers. In his poem *De Rerum Natura* the Roman poet Lucretius says:

> *Another important consideration is the diet*
> *that sustains you, for some foods make the*
> *seeds grow thick in the limbs and other foods*
> *in turn thin them and weaken them.*

In Chinese tradition, proper diet is conducive not only to bodily health but also to continued sexual activity. The Chinese too consider that excess, both in eating, and drinking, emotional anxieties, and grief are anti-aphrodisiacs.

DILL

Anethum graveolens. Used in the East for arousing desire. This herb with aromatic leaves and seeds is mentioned by the English poet Michael Drayton (1563-1630) as a stimulating ingredient in love potions.

DIONYSIA

A Greek festival in honor of Dionysus, god of wine and fertility. At the rural festival, huge phalluses were carried around in solemn public procession, symbolic of the spirit of fruitfulness. The result among the spectators was a decidedly erotic mood.

DIONYSIUS

Tyrant of Sicily. In the city of Locris he filled a house with the aphrodisiac wild thyme, and roses, and, summoning the young women of the city, he indulged in orgies with them.

DIONYSUS

Ancient god of wine and fertility. The phallus was dominant in the Dionysiac cult. In Lesbos the god was worshipped as Dionysus Phallen. In the island of Rhodes a phallic festival, the Phallophoria, was celebrated with erotic orgiastic accompaniments.

To Dionysus were dedicated the ass, the panther, the bull and the goat.

DOVE

The dove, that prolific producer of young, was known as the bird of Aphrodite. "Billing and cooing" as a metaphor for lovetalk is the language of doves. The dove is also a symbol of peace and friendship.

DRAGON'S BLOOD

A plant used as a love charm. Wrapped in paper and thrown on the fire, it was supposed to ensnare a wandering lover if this rhyming couplet was pro-

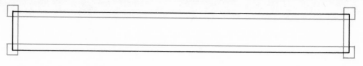

nounced over it:

May he no pleasure or profit see
Till he comes back again to me.

DREPANG: ALSO TRIPANG

A Malay term. It is a species of holothuria or sea slug, found in the Red Sea and in Oceania. On manual contact, this cucumber-shaped object expands, symbolic of an erection. Among the Arabs it is a highly popular aphrodisiac. Also greatly prized by the Chinese, to whom it is imported after the drepang is dried in the sun.

DU BARRY

Among ingredients of aphrodisiac dishes associated with Madame du Barry are ginger omelettes, stuffed capon, terrapin soup, sweetbreads, shrimp soup, crawfish.

DUDAIM

The Biblical term for mandrake. This root has been identified with various plants, roots, herbs. Some authorities equate it with raspberries, also with fruit of the Zizyphus, the Spina Christi of Linnaeus. Others attribute to it the properties of truffles.

DUFZ

A perfume used by Arabs as an aphrodisiac stimulant.

DUST

Among the Bretons of France, it was an old custom for the women to gather the dust in the chapel after religious services and blow it over a reluctant lover, in the confident expectation of the aphrodisiac effect of the action.

EELS

Like most marine life, eels are said to possess aphrodisiac properties. In this regard, eel soup is a highly favored dish.

EFFLUVIA

The power of certain aromas and odors to excite desire is evident not only in human beings, but in nearly all mammals. Most female mammals in the mating season exude peculiar emanations serving to announce to the male the presence of the female and to excite in him sexual desire. This is also true in the case of insects, for example in the female of the bombyx butterfly, which although enclosed in a hermetically sealed box, will excite and invite the approach of males. (see PHERAMONES)

EGG

It seems that the egg has been a symbol of fertility since earliest times. In France a popular aphrodisiac drink consists of the yolk of an egg in a small glass of cognac, to be drunk every morning.

Oriental dishes intended as aphrodisiacs frequently contain eggs as an ingredient.

Egg yolks are recommended by an Arab erotologist as an energetic sexual stimulant. Another potent Arab dish is a mass of eggs fried in fat and butter, then cooked and soaked in honey. This is eaten with a small piece of bread.

The Perfumed Garden says that he who eats the yolks of three eggs every day will be sexually invigorated. A similar stimulant is eggs boiled with pepper, cinnamon, and myrrh.

EGG DRINK

A highly potent drink consists of eggs, milk, salt, brandy, sugar or honey, compounded into an egg flip.

EGGPLANT

Eggplant mashed into a paste with flour and water in which bois bandé (the bark of a tree which shrinks when moistened) has been boiled and combined with peppercorns, chives, pimentos and vanilla beans was used in the West Indies as an ointment applied to the male genitals. A number of these ingredients are mild

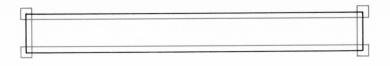

irritants which seem to enhance blood supply, thereby aiding erection.

EGG PLANT KHAJURAHO

2 small eggplants	1/2 Granny Smith apple,
1 small bunch of chives,	diced
chopped	1/2 cup butter
1/2 cup diced onion	1 sprig of parsley
1/2 cup diced celery	1 garlic clove, minced
1/2 bay leaf	1/4 tsp powdered mustard

Mix together the parsley, onion, garlic, celery, bay leaf, mustard, apple, and butter. Cook for several minutes. Stir and add the flour, mace, and curry powder and cook for another 15 minutes. Add the chicken broth and simmer for 45 minutes. Strain into a sauce pan and remove solids where possible.

Cut the eggplant into slices of equal width, approximately 1/2 inch. Add the chives to 1/2 cup of butter at room temperature. Cover both sides of the eggplant with the mixture and brown on both sides. Top with sauce.

EGYPTIAN ENTICEMENTS

To induce desire the ancient Egyptians pursued an elaborate and regular ritual. Three baths a day were a household routine, to ensure total cleanliness. The dress of the women was diaphanous, the body being veiled subtly to arouse the erotic impulse.

Depilatories were used for all hirsute parts of the body. The body was perfumed, and then treated with cosmetics. For the eyes, to enhance their glow, plant

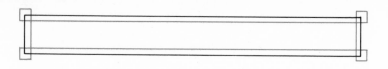

juices were applied. Finally, ornaments—gold, jewels, armlets—were added to increase the visual attraction and the sensual inclinations.

EIGHTEENTH CENTURY

Throughout Europe, especially in France and England, this century was marked as an age of licentiousness at court, among the peasantry, in poetry and on the stage. It was the age of *Tom Jones* and *Fanny Hill*, a time when the search for pleasure through aphrodisiacs and excesses of food and drink reached impassioned heights. The so-called Age of Enlightenment was also an epoch of sensual delight.

ENDIVE

Endive, like a number of similar plants, is both edible and reputed to have some aphrodisiac property. It was used as a love charm by women in Germany.

EOS

Eos, the Greek goddess of the dawn, was an unusually amorous divinity. Whoever came within her favorable and passionate notice was grasped and carried off. Such a myth, like many others popular among the Greeks, had its provocative sensual effect on the erotic inclinations of the Greeks themselves.

EROS

According to Greek mythology Eros was more than the impish son of Aphrodite, flying about with his golden arrows and making mischief with our emotions. Eros was also seen as a great demiurge, the initial power of attraction in the universe from which all subsequent life emerged. It was alternately seen as the oldest and the youngest of the deities in the Greek pantheon and ultimately came to be associated among the Greeks with homosexual rather than heterosexual love which remained the province of Aphrodite.

EROTIC DANCES

The Greek historian Herodotus describes an incident involving a sexually arousing dance. The ruler of Sicyon, Cleisthenes, had a beautiful daughter named Agariste. Numerous suitors appeared in turn, all unsuccessfully. Then Hippoclides appeared, a wealthy young Athenian. Having drunk heavily, Hippoclides mounted the table and performed a number of lewd dances. Cleisthenes, shocked, exclaimed, "You have danced away your bride."

EROTIC FESTIVAL

In ancient Greece, the five-day festival of the Thesmophoria was celebrated by women only, in honor of the goddesses Persephone and Demeter. This was symbolically a propagation rite and involved women, married life, and childbearing. In the course of time the festival spread through all the colonies of Greece, to Sicily, the shores of the Black Sea, and Asia Minor.

In Attica, the women participants were required to observe sexual abstinence for nine days before the festival. The ostensible reason, said the priests, was an act of piety, but actually the abstinence increased sexual appetites that were satisfied during the festival.

Erotic Provocations

The Arab erotologist Sheik Nefzawi says:

The kiss on the mouth, on the two cheeks, upon the neck, as well as the sucking up of fresh lips, are gifts of God.

These amatory expressions, he adds, provoke further activity.

Erotic Religious Mysteries

At Paphos in Cyprus, a Greek festival was held annually in honor of Aphrodite, goddess of love. Men and women participated in the ceremonies, which were characterized by orgiastic rites.

The initiated member gave a gift of a coin for the goddess, for which he received in turn a phallus and some salt.

Erotic Sale

In the ancient city of Isernia, in the Kingdom of Naples, as late as the eighteenth century an annual three-day fair was held. At this festival wax reproductions of the male genitalia were publicly exposed for sale. These images were usually purchased by barren women as a hopeful means of encouraging conception.

Erotic Symbols

To Aphrodite, goddess of love in ancient mythology, the ram, the hare, the dove, the sparrow and the goat were all sacred. Their significance lay in the fact that they all had particularly amorous natures, so that in a more generalized sense, whatever promoted the concept of prolific sexual expression was welcome and dedicated to the goddess. The prevalence of this notion was so widespread that the coins of Cyprus presented the image of the ram.

In Athens, the goddess was known as Aphrodite Epitragia (that is, Aphrodite on a Goat).

In the goddess' temples doves were kept and cared for by the attendants.

In the Roman novelist Apuleius' *Metamorphoses* Aphrodite rides in a car drawn by four doves, with an accompaniment of sparrows and other birds.

In a poem by Sappho, Aphrodite is represented as riding in a car drawn by sparrows.

EROTIC TALES

Every age has its literary erotic stimulants to whet the popular appetite or to imprint in permanence the basic ethnic legends that center around the primary and universal procreative principle. Sometimes these sagas and anecdotes are touched with ribaldry, or with excessive obscenity according to the times, and sometimes they are rooted in obscure but still verifiable deistic concepts.

Among the Greeks, the tales of Pherecydes of Syros, of which only fragments still exist, the digressive anecdotes in Herodotus' *History of the Persian Wars*, the collection entitled *Milesian Tales* produced by

Aristides of the first century B.C. and the love romance narrated by Ctesias the physician are among the significant contributions to the erotic genre. Among the Romans, the famous picaresque novel of the *Satyricon*, by Petronius, as well as the adventurous and libidinous *Metamorphoses* of Apuleius, are particularly notable. Later ages contributed in their own manner to these universal delights in the erotic. In China, *The Golden Lotus* is an amazing achievement.

Boccaccio's *Decameron* in Italy, *The Arabian Nights* in the Moslem world, Walter Map's *De Nugis Curialium*, especially the tale of the two merchants, and the Turkish folk tales with their wild buffoon-like but shrewd protagonist have become incorporated in the stream of world literature. France added a not inconsiderable quota. Restif de la Bretonne produced *Les Contemporains*, early in the nineteenth century.

Paul de Kock, who died in 1871, followed with a large number of erotic tales, of which *La Pucelle de Belleville* was a characteristic example. The *Contes Drólatiques* of Honore de Balzac and the *Contes Cruels* of Villiers de L'Isle-Adam all testify to man's continuous interest and absorption in erotic matters.

ERYNGO

Eryngium maritimum is an herb also known as Sea Holly, Sea Hulver, and Sea Holme. It has the appearance of a thistle with blue flowers. For centuries its root was used as powerful aphrodisiac. It is still used as a condiment for the same purpose.

Eryngos grew wild along the coast of England and Shakespeare mentions them as an aphrodisiac in *The Merry Wives of Windsor*. Even the renowned Lord Bacon recommended them in combination with wine and malmsey as a good restorative for the back.

During Elizabethan times, when this herb enjoyed its highest reputation, an enterprising fellow named Robert Burton opened a factory for the production of "kissing comfits"—candied roots of the eryngo that restored the liver as well as youthful masculine vigor.

The Arabs knew it in this candied form as an invigorating stimulant for both men and women.

EXCESS

In reference to loss of virility and sexual excesses, Nefzawi, the author of *The Perfumed Garden*, asserts:

> *All sages and physicians agree in saying that the ills which afflict man originate with the abuse of coition. The man therefore who wishes to preserve his health, and particularly his sight, and who wants to lead a pleasant life, will indulge with moderation in love's pleasures, aware that the greatest evils may spring therefrom.*

EXCESS OF APHRODISIACS

Sickness and even death not infrequently resulted from excessive doses of philtres and other aphrodisiac

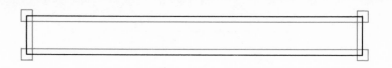

treatments. A courtesan once prepared a lavish dinner for a passionate young man. Every dish was spiced with the notorious cantharides, or Spanish fly. The guest, partaking eagerly of the feast, died the next day.

EXTERNAL APPLICATIONS

Liniments and other applications have been used externally to stimulate the libido. These washes and preparations were made of honey, liquid storax, oil, fresh butter, or the fat of the wild goose, together with a small quantity of spurge, pyrethrum, ginger, or pepper, with the further addition of a few grains of ambergris, musk, or cinnamon. The manual stimulation along with the mild irritants increased blood flow, sensation, and therefore, erection and excitement.

EYE

The Greeks, especially the dramatists Aeschylus, Sophocles, and Euripides, considered the eye the gateway to love. Hence the marked effects of visual aphrodisiac representations on the beholder.

FENNEL

A fragrant plant used in sauces and believed to inspire sexual activity.

A Hindu prescription for sexual vigor and at the same time a preservative of health contains these ingredients: Juice of the fennel plant and milk mixed with honey, ghee, liquorice, and sugar. This compound is described as holy, partaking of the essence of nectar.

Fennel soup is a dish used in some Mediterranean regions, reputed to stimulate desire.

FIGS

Figs were anciently associated with sexual symbolism. Plutarch, the Greek biographer and philosopher, has this to say:

*The festival of the Dionysia was anciently
celebrated in a popular and lively manner. A
wine-jar was carried round and also a vine-
branch. Then someone brought forward a
goat, and another a basket filled with figs;
and over all the phallus.*

The fig was also symbolic of the male and female sex
organs. The French expression *faire la figue* means to
make the obscene sexual gesture with two fingers and
thumb. This gesture was well-known in the antique
lupanaria of the Romans.

FISH

Traditionally considered a powerful and unfailing
erotic aid, particularly because of the presence of
phosphates and iodine.

Catherine II of Russia, childless with her husband, the
grandson of Peter the Great, was told by her Chancel-
lor that the Empire urgently required an heir. Impe-
rialistic and realistic, Catherine ordered some caviar,
and commanded her chef to prepare a fine sturgeon.
Saltikoff, an officer of the guard, was to be invited to
dinner. The outcome of her forthright gastronomic
decision was a healthy, acceptable heir.

Another historical anecdote, whether apocryphal or
not: Saladin, to test the celibacy of some dervishes,
invited two of them to his palace, and entertained
them with rich food. They grew fat, but successfully

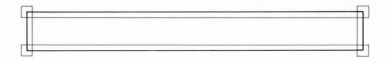

resisted the enticing women with whom they were confronted.

Surprised, Saladin changed the menu, serving only fish, excellently prepared, to the dervishes. Introduced once again to the charmers, this time they succumbed.

Of particular interest as stimuli are carp, lobster, caviar, and all kinds of roe, eel, salmon, mullet, tunny, herring, mackerel, plaice, whiting, and halibut.

In Egypt the aphrodisiac virtues of fish were so generally recognized that priests were forbidden to eat fish.

In antiquity, fish were credited with special aphrodisiac virtues and efficacy in exciting women. A suggested explanation was that Venus herself was born of the sea. Her Greek name, Aphrodite, is associated with the Greek term *aphros*, which means foam.

FLOUNDER FILLET FANDANGO

2 flounder fillets, 3/4 lb. each, sliced thin	1/2 cup seedless green grapes
1/4 cup mayonnaise	1/2 cup seedless red grapes
1/4 cup dill	

Cut the grapes in half. Brush both sides of the flounder with mayonnaise. Sprinkle with dill. Broil fillets for 5 minutes on one side. Add the grapes decoratively to the fillets and broil for another 3 minutes. Serve with rice and a small green salad.

FLOWERS

The aroma given off by flowers often has an aphrodi-

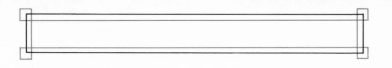

siac effect, especially on women. This is so particularly in the case of lilies of the valley, gardenia, frangipane, and henna.

FRANGIPANE CREAM
A pastry consisting of frangipane (or red jasmine), spices and almonds, is recommended as a sexual aid in an Italian erotic cookery manual.

FRANKINCENSE
This is the perfume known also as olibanum. It is frequently mentioned in Biblical contexts, usually in association with erotic themes. (see OLIBANUM)

FROGS
Frogs, and the bones of frogs, were used as aphrodisiacs by the Romans.

FROGS' LEGS
In many countries treated as a culinary delicacy, especially in France, and known as a "noble aphrodisiac."

FRUIT
Among fruits reputed to have stimulating qualities are bananas, fresh figs, peaches, cherries, grapes.

GALANGA

An Indian root used among Arabs as an aphrodisiac:

> *A compound of galanga, cubebs, sparrow*
> *wort, cardamoms, nutmeg, gillyflowers,*
> *Indian thistle, laurel seeds, cloves, Persian*
> *pepper is made into a drink. Taken twice*
> *daily morning and night, in pigeon or fowl*
> *broth, preceded and followed by water.*

The result, according to Arab tradition, is an effective aphrodisiac.

GALL

The bile of a jackal, among Arabs, was used as an aphrodisiac. It is specifically recommended as an ointment for this purpose by the Sheik Nefzawi, author of *The Perfumed Garden*.

GAME

Goose, duck, and pheasant are all credited with being stimulants in an erotic sense.

GARLIC

Of reputed aphrodisiac value, according to medical authority. Both European and Oriental erotologists include garlic as an aphrodisiac ingredient in foods.

Among the Ainu of Japan garlic was considered in the same category as the ancient Greek nectar and ambrosia of the gods.

GENEANTHROPOEIA

A comprehensive textbook, in Latin, that is in the nature of a course in sexology and anatomy. The author is Johannes Benedict Sinibaldus, an Italian professor of medicine who published the book in Rome in 1642. Many chapters in the book deal with aphrodisiacs, especially from an historical viewpoint and also contain numerous warnings against excessive sexual activity.

GENITAL ADORNMENTS

Among some primitive tribal communities in East Indian islands and in South America, the men adorn the *membrum virile* with trinkets, rings, shells, and similar objects.

GENTIAN WINE

Considered to have an aphrodisiac virtue and often, in a particularly erotic atmosphere, it has that property.

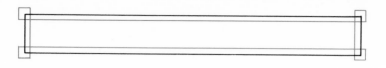

GHEE

In Hindu practice, ghee, which is clarified butter, is considered an aphrodisiac.

A Hindu manual of erotology suggests boiled ghee, drunk on spring mornings, as a healthful, strengthening beverage.

GEORGE IV

This English king so highly appreciated the virtues of truffles, that he gave his Foreign Ministers special directions. His Ministers at the Courts of Turin, Naples, Florence, were emphatically counseled to forward to the Royal Kitchen any truffles that might be found superior in size, delicacy, or flavor.

GINGER

Long known and used in the Far and Middle East in the native dietary.

Often used for medicinal purposes in China. A ginger-fruit jam is made among the Chinese and is credited with active sexual properties.

In Turkish, Indian, Arabian and other Oriental love recipes, ginger is frequently present as an ingredient in amatory concoctions, often taken by mouth along with honey and pepper.

GINSENG

The root of *Panax ginseng* grows in Korea and China where it has long been known medicinally. The root resembles the male body, hence the association with potency in the restoration of virility.

In scientific studies it has been shown that ginseng does have some efficacy in increasing physical and intellectual stamina. It contains many minerals as well as B vitamins. The Russians gave their astronauts extract of Siberian ginseng to strengthen them.

Its use as an aphrodisiac is not proven beyond its capacity to enhance the general state of well-being and vigor. However, the Indians of North America used it extensively for sexual stimulation and the Chinese Taoists believed it enhanced the proper balance and exchange of sexual energy between men and women.

GOAT

In ancient times, the goat was associated with the goddess Aphrodite and Dionysus, the god of fertility and procreation, because of its amorous tendencies. Pan, the sylvan deity who was attended by the satyrs, was invariable represented with goat's feet and was the special protector of goats.

GOSSYPION

A tree whose juice, according to a medieval writer named Andreas Cisalpinus, was esteemed as an aphrodisiac.

GOUROU

The native African term for the kola nut. This is really a large chestnut, like a horse chestnut. The natives of Senegal and the Sudan chew the gourou with delight, says an anthropologist, although it has a sharp and astringent taste. It produces a sort of general nervous excitement, increasing all the physical faculties, including of course, the generative powers.

At the great *bamboulas* and fêtes the gourou is heavily used. It is a most valuable fruit when exceptionally hard work (amorous or otherwise) has to be done, but its use should not be abused.

Kola is now admitted into European therapeutics, and is used for restoring lost strength and stimulating the forces of the body. It contains a great quantity of caffeine and theobromine than the best teas and coffees.

GRAHAM

In the eighteenth century a certain Dr. James Graham, a charlatan who claimed to be an alchemist, described in his public lectures various fantastic aphrodisiacal remedies. He exhorted his audience thusly:

> *Suffer me, with great cordiality, and assurance of success, to recommend my celestial, or medico, magnetico, musico, electrical bed which I have constructed...to improve, exalt, and invigorate the bodily, and through them, the mental faculties of the human species....*
>
> *The sublime, the magnificent, and, I may say, the supercelestial dome of the bed, which contains the odoriferous, balmy, and ethereal spices, odors and essences, and which is the grand magazine or reservoir of those vivifying and invigorating influences which are exhaled and dispersed by the breathing of the music,*

and by the attenuating, repelling, and accelerating force of the electrical fire—is very curiously inlaid or wholly covered on the underside with brilliant plates of looking-glass, so disposed as to reflect the various attractive charms of the happy recumbent couple, in the most flattering, most agreeable, and most enchanting style.

Such is a slight and inadequate sketch of the grand celestial bed, which, fully impregnated with the balmy effluvia of restorative balsamic medicines and of soft, fragrant, oriental gums, balsams, and quintessence, and pervaded at the same time with full springing tides of the invigorating influences of music and magnets both real and artificial, gives such elastic vigor to the nerves, on the one hand, of the male, and on the other, such retentive firmness to the female...that it is impossible, in the nature of things, but that strong, beautiful, brilliant, nay, double-distilled children, if I may use the expression, must be begotten.

Dr. Graham's bed measured nine by twelve feet and cost 10,000 pounds to build. The not inconsiderable rental fee included an orchestra to serenade the couple.

GRAPES

In ancient times grapes were associated with the god Dionysus, deity of fertility and procreation and the wine that accompanied his uninhibited worship.

HALIBUT

This fish is considered to have particularly strong aphrodisiac properties.

HALLUCINOGENS

A group of drugs that produce colorful visions and hallucinations, magnifying all forms of sensation. The drugs in this class may produce aphrodisiac effects by means of erotic visions and by the magnification of sensations. These visions occur with a marked sexual flavor, and an increased sensuality.

These drugs are derivatives of plants and may have aphrodisiac results. Among them are yohombine, mescaline, nux vomica under certain conditions, rauwiloid, and brucine.

HARE SOUP

The hare has a reputation for exciting desire, proba-

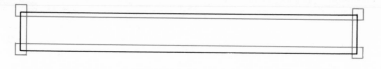

bly related to the vast number of offspring it produces. Hare soup is credited with exceptional aphrodisiac value.

HASHISH

An Indian hemp plant, *cannabis indica*. In Arabic it means "dried herb." The term "assassin" is derived from the Arabic *hashishin*, or "hemp eaters," that is, drug addicts.

Among Morrocans a compound consisting of hashish, acorns, honey, sweet almonds, sesame, butter, cantharides (Spanish fly), and nuts is a popular aphrodisiac.

The aphrodisiac properties attributed to hashish and marijuana are indirect at best and are related more to the general relaxing of inhibitions and the increased suggestibility of the user. In fact, sustained use of either drug leads to decrease in desire. For this reason, hashish was used by monks and friars in the East to decrease sexual feelings. Theophile Gautier, the nineteenth century French poet and novelist, was a hashish addict who declared that "a hashish addict would not lift a finger for the most beautiful maiden in Verona."

HEMP

Among the Turks, pills consisting of hemp buds, muscat nuts, saffron, and honey were a popular aphrodisiac.

HENNA

The pulverized leaves and twigs of this plant are used as a hair dye in European countries and the East.

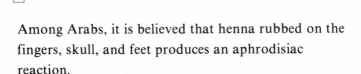

Among Arabs, it is believed that henna rubbed on the fingers, skull, and feet produces an aphrodisiac reaction.

HERBS

Among herbs that have traditionally been considered to possess aphrodisiac virtue are maidenhair fern, navelwort, anemone, wild poppy, valerian, cyclamen, male fern, pansy, periwinkle, black pepper, cardamom, jasmine, juniper, rose, and sandalwood.

HERISSAH

In the Orient, a concoction of mutton and flour seasoned with red pepper was believed to be a sexual stimulant.

HERMES

In Greek cities the god Hermes was commemorated by the presence in public of numerous Hermes pillars. These were stone pillars surmounted by a head representing the god himself and a phallus. Mercury is the name of the Roman counterpart of Hermes.

HERRING

Like most species of fish, herring are considered to have considerable aphrodisiac virtue.

HETAIRA

The Greek word for courtesan. These Greek and Roman practitioners of the art of love made aphrodisiacs with pepper, myrrh, two perfumes called Cyprian and Egyptian and other substances that were believed to stimulate desire.

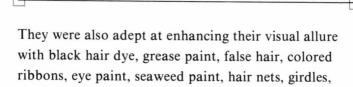

They were also adept at enhancing their visual allure with black hair dye, grease paint, false hair, colored ribbons, eye paint, seaweed paint, hair nets, girdles, combs and necklaces, and many other adornments.

HIERODOULOI

Sexual indulgence was, in many countries including ancient Greece, virtually a religious duty consistent with the worship of the goddess of love. Hence it is easy to appreciate the religious status of the hierodouloi, the sacred temple priestesses who celebrated the rites of love and were well-versed in its art. Their purpose was to bring about the *hierogamos* or "sacred marriage" between the two creative, procreative energies of male and female.

The temple of Aphrodite of Byblos in Phoenicia was noted for these special priestesses as was the cult of Mylitta in Babylonia. In Cyprus the hierodouloi of the temples at Amathos and Paphos were dedicated to Aphrodite Astarte. Their counterparts in Rome at the temple of Venus Erycina enjoyed a widespread reputation.

The sacred priestess of love was equally an institution in ancient Semitic kingdoms and was known as *q'desha*. The Old Testament contains a number of references to them as practicing idolatry.

HINDU APHRODISIACS

Onions, beans, garlic, and leeks are constantly mentioned as conducive to sexual activity in epic literature, as is the eating of meat. Heady drinks and festivals enlivened with music are said to promote erotic designs. Among the recommended drinks are mad-hirka which is extracted from flowers, and mad-humadhavi which is made from honey.

The Hindus also list the beauties of nature as muses of love: the wind in springtime, the humming of bees, flowers budding and the songs of birds.

It was claimed by the Greek encyclopedist Athenaeus that some Indian aphrodisiacs were so powerful that, if applied to the soles of the feet, they immediately increased passion.

HINDU IDEAL

In some respects, Hindu ideals of feminine perfection coincide with those of Arab countries. The face should be as pleasing as the new moon. The body should be soft as the mustard flower. A fine, fair, tender skin is a requisite as well as eyes bright as those of a fawn, bosom full and firm, the nose straight, a swan-like gliding gait, the voice low and musical, while the garments should be white, flowing, adorned with jewels.

HINDU PASSION

In Hindu tradition, the sexual energies were highly regarded as the embodiment of the creative, procrea-tive elements of the universe. They were open to stim-ulation by all the five senses.

HINDU POWDER

According to one of the famous manuals, eating the

powder of the *nelumbrium speciosum*, the blue lotus, and the *mesna roxburghii*, with ghee and honey is an effective amatory enticement.

HIPPOCRAS APHRODISIAC

According to folk tradition, a potent sexual stimulant. It consists of red Burgundy wine with an admixture of ginger, crushed cinnamon, cloves, vanilla, and white sugar. Rabelais, in *Gargantua and Pantagruel*, refers to its healthful value:

> *Then shall you be presented with a cup of claret hypocras, which is right healthful and stomachal.*

HIPPOCRATES

Hippocrates, the most famous Greek physician, who died in the same year as Socrates, in 399 B.C., declared that a predisposing cause of impotence among the ancient Scythians was the wearing of breeches. Arab erotologists express similar views about more modern conditions.

HIPPOMANES

A protuberance that supposedly appears on a colt's head at birth and that is bitten off by the mare. Hippomanes was used in ancient Roman potions as an aphrodisiac. It was as large as a fig, black in color, and derived its name from a Greek expression meaning horse-madness.

Vergil, Ovid, Pliny the Elder and Juvenal all describe

hippomanes as an excrescence on a new-born colt. In the Aeneid, Vergil, listing the operations of a witch-priestess, says:

She has sprinkled water, so she feigns, from Avernus' spring and she is getting green downy herbs cropped by moonlight with brazen shears, whose sap is the milk of deadly poison, and the love-charm, torn from the brow of the new-born foal ere the mother could snatch it.

HONEY

In Oriental dishes intended as aphrodisiacs, honey is a frequent ingredient.

Galen, a Greek of the second century A.D., court physician to the Emperor Marcus Aurelius, recommended as an effective aphrodisiac a glass of thick honey, taken before bedtime, together with the consumption of almonds and one hundred grains of the pine tree. The recipe was to be followed for three successive days.

A compound of honey, pepper, and ginger is recommended as an aphrodisiac by the thirteenth century Arab physician Avicenna.

HORSERADISH

As a condiment, reputed to have a stimulating sexual value.

IDEAL

The Arabs have their own ethnic standards of female beauty, the cumulative presence of which, in any particular woman, would inspire the most extreme feelings.

This ideal includes a body white as ivory, teeth like rice in whiteness and glow, the gait and step of a young spirited mare or doe. This ideal woman's hair is black, and hangs in thick tresses. Her lashes are curved, her breasts firm, her hips wide.

In figure she should stand upright, like a palm tree that grows skyward in the oasis. With her narrow waist, and perfumed with myrrh, and adorned with tinkling jewelry, she can allure any man by her seductive presence without the aid of any other contrived aphrodisiacs.

INTESTINES

The intestines of fish and birds were used as aphrodi-

siacs among the Romans.

ITALIAN PLANT

In Italy, a plant called *Pizza ugurdu* is said to excite powerful erotic feelings even in the most frigid. It has been identified with the Greek *Vorax*.

ITALIAN STIMULI

Among the aphrodisiac ingredients listed in a manual of erotic cookery are basil, snakeroot, soup seasoned with cloves, laurel, truffles, celery, thyme, parsley, fennel, artichoke, chocolate.

ITHYPHALLUS

The Latin word for erection, from the Greek root *ithyphallikos*. It is used to refer to the large phalluses carried in ancient festivals worshipping the god Bacchus, and to the hymns sung in these solemn processions.

The eternal object yet unattained—one of the major quests of the erotically inclined—the infinitely long-lasting erection. All sorts of bizarre and complicated preparations have been concocted in every age and in every country, it seems, in pursuit of this elusive goal. These preparations include oils, powders, brews, unguents, electuaries, charms, mechanical contrivances, incantations, and occult supplications. Perceived as the source not only of pleasure but also of progeny, men and women all through the ages have sought out witches and warlocks, sex therapists, doctors and shamans for help and we'll probably never stop.

JEALOUSY

Jealousy has been considered an indirect sexual stimulant.

In one of the Greek satirist Lucian's *Dialogues of Courtesans*, a conversation takes place between the hetaira Tryphaena and a young client named Charmides. Tryphaena arouses the visitor to a frenzied pitch of amorous activity by describing the faded realities of Charmides' previous object of passion, a certain Philemation.

JUNIPER

A shrub that produces fleshy berries of purple color and pungent taste. Yields an oil used medicinally. The berries are steeped in water and the juice is drunk. John Gerarde, author of *Herball* which he wrote in

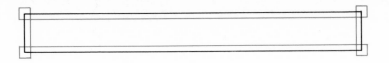

1633, recommends it as a wholesome drink. Juniper is also credited with the virtue of successfully maintaining youthful ardor.

Often used as an ingredient in cordials, juniper was formerly considered of medicinal value by herbalists. It was also a common ingredient in love philtres.

JUNO

Juno represents the union of the feminine and masculine energies of the universe through the sacred marriage manifested in Tantric sexual rites. This conjoining occurs on the most abstract and esoteric levels as well as on the more familiar and physical ones.

The wife of Zeus/Jupiter, she frequently expressed her anger toward her mate's infidelities. As keeper of the committed relationship, she is its protector and signifies the transition from a focus on self to a focus on relatedness, both to a single partner, to children and to the larger community.

KALLIPYGIAN COQUETRY

In other words, the provocative, sensuous motion of the hips as in hula, belly dancing, and the subtle or not so subtle sway of a woman's walk (or a man's for that matter).

The ancient Greek writer Hesiod inveighed against these actions by single women and wives as coquettish and vain. He was known as a misogynist.

KALOGYNOMIA

The Laws of Female Beauty. A book on love techniques, rules of intercourse, prostitution, infidelity, together with a catalogue of female defects. Published in London, in 1821. The author was a certain Dr. T. Bell.

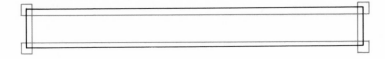

KAMA SUTRA

A Sanskrit manual of erotic procedures written by Vatsyayana. This comprehensive text dealing with all aspects of love and sex has been translated into English by Sir Richard Burton, the noted Orientalist. The following is a prescription for an effective stimulant:

Cut into small pieces the sprouts of the vajnasunhi plant, dip into a mixture of red arsenic and sulphur, dry seven times. Burn this powder at night and observe the smoke. If a golden moon is visible behind the fumes, the amatory experience will be successful.

In addition to offering specific formulas and prescriptions for inducing desire, the *Kama Sutra* advises consultation with the family when sexual problems arise, the reading of the Sanskrit Vedas, and visits to physicians and magicians.

It is also forthright in warning against injurious and impure concoctions and items that are destructive to animal life. It recommended for use as aphrodisiacs only those objects beneficial and acceptable to the Brahmans, or priest class.

Kama Sutra itself means "Aphorisms on Love." There are some twelve hundred verses, ranging in great detail over all aspects of love and dwelling particularly on aphrodisiac aids.

All directions and counsel given in the *Kama Sutra* stress that the prudent, intelligent man will, instead of

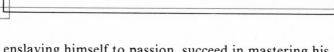

enslaving himself to passion, succeed in mastering his senses.

KANTAKA

The *Kama Sutra* suggests that to increase vigor a certain mixture be thrown at the woman in question. It is compounded of the powder of the milk hedge plant and kantaka plant, combined with monkey excrement and the powdered root of the lanjalika plant. This prescription may actually belong under the heading of anti-aphrodisiacs.

KAVA PIPERACEAE

A plant found in the entire area of the South Sea Islands. The roots produce a liqueur called kava. Kava has a mild aphrodisiac effect. The Polynesian natives drink kava after wedding ceremonies and are evidently stimulated by it.

Kava drink is made by chewing the root of the pepper plant and spitting it into a kava bowl. The drink is then strained and served in a coconut cup.

KISSING

Kissing is essentially a sexual act leading to the intimacy resulting in erotic consummation.

This is the view of the celebrated Roman poet Ovid who wrote the *Ars Amatoria*. He declares that the man who has stolen a kiss and does not know how to steal the rest deserves to lose his advantage.

LAMPREY

This eel-like pseudo-fish is said to increase the seminal fluid.

LARD

Lard mixed with crushed and strained garlic has been used as a sexually stimulating ointment.

LAUREL LEAVES

Laurel leaves were used in the Orient to promote sexual arousal.

LAVENDER

Small doses of lavender are said to cause excitation. A few flowers in tobacco induce a dream-like state.

LE CHANSONNIER BACHIQUE DE L'AMOUR ET DE LA FOLIE

A collection of French songs intended for banquets, weddings and similar occasions. Published by a society of gourmets in Paris, in 1816. They created the

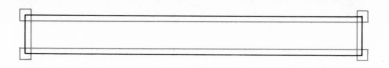

proper convivial and erotic atmosphere. Since antiquity, especially among the Greeks and the Romans, obscenities, lubricities, and erotic activity have been associated with the sense of euphoria stimulated by gastonomic plentitude and diversions.

LECITHIN

This nitrogenous fatty substance that appears in certain foods is considered an element in inducing sexual desire.

LENTILS

In ancient Greece, lentils were believed to stimulate desire. (see BEANS)

LIÉBAULT, JEAN

(c. 1535-1596). A French sexologist, native of Dijon and member of the Faculty of Medicine in Paris. Author of *Thrésor des Remèdes pour Les Maladies des Femmes*. It is an encyclopedia of sexual knowledge as it was known in his time.

He makes detailed suggestions on the means of strengthening sexual vigor, analyzing conditions as organic or psychological, and advising in accordance with each specific condition. In a general sense, he recommends as a stimulus a sound and wholesome diet, special foods and drinks, along with electuaries and ointments, massage and similar exercises whose purpose is to reinforce erotic feelings and tendencies. He enumerates, in a long list of recipes and prescrip-

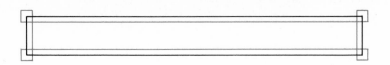

tions: disatyrion and dates, nuts, figs, wine in moderation, ointments applied to the body, game, fresh fish cooked in onions, pomegranates. A warm bath is a pleasant stimulant, to be followed by a period of sleep. Chestnuts are advisable, also chicken soup, mutton, lamb, veal prepared in special ways, fatted suckling pigs. Most dishes have their own sauces. Spices in great variety are listed: cardamom, long pepper, ginger, cubebs, saffron, cinnamon, galanga. These spices may be used on meats and in pastry. Rice cooked in milk of sheep is advised as a potent aid. Also, certain pharmaceutical items that were in common use in the seventeenth century.

In addition, beyond all mechanical, gastronomic, and external aids, there should be amatory talk, erotic thoughts, exercise in the peripheral erotic advances, as well as tactile contacts. All these procedures, Liébault advises, should produce the desired consummation.

LINGAM PREPARATIONS

In the famous Hindu guide to erotology, the *Ananga-Ranga*, a number of ointments that will create and prolong erection are recommended. They include among their ingredients anise, honey, leaves of the aji, rui seed, Hungarian grass, and lotus pollen.

LINIMENTS

A seventeenth century erotologist lists the following ingredients among unguents and liniments that have active sexual impact: honey, goose fat, butter, storax, ghee, spurge, chives, musk, ginger, ambergris, and pepper.

LION'S FAT

Lion's fat is listed as a favorite medieval aphrodisiac treatment in the *Geneanthropoeia*.

LIQUEURS

Many liqueurs, among them chartreuse and benedictine, have long been held in great esteem as aphrodisiac aids.

LIVER

According to the Roman poet Horace, liver was popular in his day as an aphrodisiac.

LIZARD

Lizards are favored in Arab countries for their reputed power to enhance erotic experience. An Arab recipe for potency consists of Chinese cubebs (a kind of pepper), cloves, cinnamon, Roumi opium, ginger, cardamom, mountain lizard, and white pepper pounded together and boiled in sweet olive oil. Male frankincense is added, and coriander seed. The entire composition is then macerated and mixed with honey. Taken after supper, it is to be washed down with rose conserve sherbert.

By itself, the lizard is powdered and drunk with sweet wine, acting as an aphrodisiac. When held in the hand, the lizard supposedly produces an amorous stimulus.

In Egypt, lizards were brought to Cairo by Egyptian fellahin, then shipped to Mediterranean ports, particularly Marseilles, and also Venice, where they were

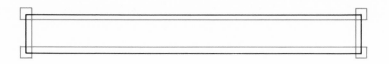

much sought after.

LOCALIZED PERFUMES

Among the Arabs, who are highly sensitive to aromas as sexual stimulants, perfume is applied for this purpose to the mouth, under the arms, to the nose and the female genitalia.

LOVE AND BE LOVED

According to some authorities on sexology and related fields, the most effective and most natural aphrodisiac is the passion itself for the object of love. That passion, intense and prolonged, should be sufficient under normal conditions to achieve all necessary amatory consummations.

Ovid, the Roman poet who wrote *Ars Amatoria*, says,

> *To be loved, be lovable.*

This definitive and succinct injunction is repeated by Seneca, another distinguished Roman philosopher. He declares,

> *I will show you a philtre without potions, without herbs, without amy witch's incantation—if you wish to be loved, love.*

LOVE CHARM

Such devices have always been popular, particularly in the Orient. In India, women use a variety of charms and amulets to inspire or retain passion in their lovers. (see CHARMS)

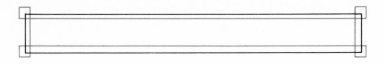

LOVE FEAST

On the island of Cyprus the birth and first manifestation of the goddess Aphrodite were elaborated into a celebration at which all the people gathered. The goddess' image was bathed in the sea by women and girls, then decked with garlands. Bathing in the river followed, culminating in love orgies, the preceding formalities being, in a sense, introductory stimulants.

LOVE NESTS

In ancient Greece, at Cnidus and Olympia and elsewhere, there were pandokeia, *inns*, that ostensibly constituted shelters for visitors and travelers but in practice were haunts for sexual enjoyments.

LOVE ROMANCES

Among a number of Greek erotic tales that have come down to us are the story of Chaereas and Kallirrhoe, by Chariton who lived in the second century A.D., and the love of Abrocomes and Antheia, by Xenophon of Ephesus. Heliodorus of Emesa produced the story of Theagenes and Chariclea. Longus of Lesbos is the author of the romance of Daphnis and Chloe.

LOZENGES

In ancient times, perfumed lozenges and pastilles were widely sold as aphrodisiac aids. They were called, appropriately enough, *avunculae Cypriae*—the Aunts of the Cyprian Goddesses (Venus).

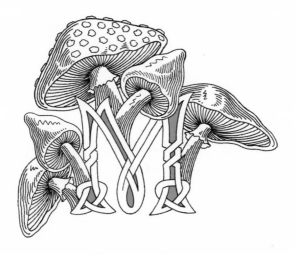

MACKEREL

Another fish said to enhance energy and desire.

MALLOWS

The root of mallow in goat's milk excites the sexual urge, according to Pliny the Elder, the Roman encyclopedist of the first century A.D. If the root was eaten dry, on the other hand, it was believed to act as an anti-aphrodisiac.

The sap of mallows, together with three mallow roots tied together, aroused the passions of a woman, according to the same writer.

MANDRAKE

The legendary powers of the mandrake to enflame desire and aid fertility are noted in many cultures around the world including classical Greece and Rome, China, India, and it is mentioned a number of times in the Old Testament.

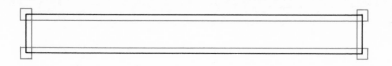

The actual plant is the *atropa mandragora* and belongs to the potato family. It has dark leaves with purple flowers, tomato-like fruit and is indigenous to the Mediterranean area, especially the Middle Eastern areas.

Its root often grows in a human-like shape which has certainly contributed to the legends and lore celebrating it as an aphrodisiac. However, there is no evidence that it has any such effect. What it does possess are certain alkaloids that induce sleep and it has been used for centuries as a soporific and for general anesthesia. Beyond the loosening of our inhibitions when we are drowsy and relaxed, the mandrake has no direct aphrodisiac effects.

The mandrake of myth and legend is quite different. The ancient Homeric witch Circe used it in her magic brews, hence the root was known as "the plant of Circe".

One of the love goddess's names is Aphrodite Mandragoritis, "She of the Mandrake".

In the Middle Ages quacks often played on the credulity of the ignorant populace at fairs and markets by exhibiting rudely carved figures that they claimed to be mandrakes that would aid in conception. A sixteenth century monograph on witch craft exposed the procedure:

> *Imposters carve the male and female forms*
> *upon these plants while yet green, inserting*
> *millet or barley seeds in such parts as they*

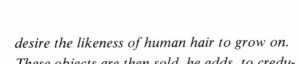

desire the likeness of human hair to grow on.
These objects are then sold, he adds, to credu-
lous peasants and love-sick men and maidens.

Up until the nineteenth century, young Greeks carried pieces of mandrake with them in their satchels as love-charms.

MANGO

The following treatment is suggested in Hindu eroto-logical literature as a stimulant: "Arris root, dressed with oil of mango. Place in a hole in the trunk of the sisu tree for six months. Remove and make into an ointment for application to the genitals."

MARIJUANA

Marijuana is a relative of hashish, its scientific name is *cannabis sativa*. Like hashish, it is an aphrodisiac only indirectly. Like all drugs, continued use diminishes rather than enhances sexual desire and performance. (see HASHISH)

MARJORAM

An aromatic herb used in flavoring foods. Believed to have aphrodisiac properties.

MARROW

Traditionally, bone marrow is a source of vitality. Hence a paté of marrow was a common concoction for whetting amorous appetites.

The Roman poet Horace refers to dried marrow as a regular aphrodisiac.

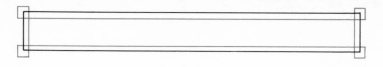

MARZIPAN

A slice of marzipan followed by a drink of hippocras is an aphrodisiac prescription advised by Rabelais in his *Gargantua and Pantagruel*.

MASSAGE

Massage, particularly in the inguinal area, was frequently resorted to by the ancients as an inducement to potency. The practice is mentioned often in Greek literature.

MASTIC

An Arab aphrodisiac. A drink made from the fruit of the mastic tree, pounded with honey and oil, was recommended for increasing sperm.

MATHEMATICS

It has been at least an academic tradition, if no more, that mathematical studies militate against sexual arousal.

MEAT

Although Hindu religious customs proscribed the eating of meat, meat was believed to increase sexual power and is often mentioned in this respect in Hindu sexological manuals. Lean, red meat in particular is credited with strong aphrodisiac effects.

MEDIEVAL ANECDOTE

Brasica eruca, a kind of cabbage, sown in the garden of a monastery was taken as a daily infusion by the monks who believed that it would cheer and rouse them from customary sluggishness. But the continued

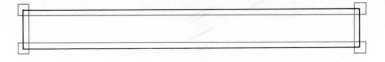

use of it produced such an aphrodisiac effect that the cenobites, as the chronicle relates, transgressed alike.

MEDIEVAL REMEDY

A fourteenth century remedy for impotence that has been contrived through magic spells is as follows:

> "*Burdock seeds, pounded in a mortar. Add the left testis of a three-year old goat, a pinch of powder from the back hairs of a dog that is entirely white. The hairs to be cut on the first day of the new moon and burned on the seventh day. Infuse all these items in a bottle half filled with brandy. Leave uncorked for 21 days, so that it may receive the astral influence.*
>
> "*On the 21st day—that is, precisely the first of the following moon—cook the entire compound until a thick consistency is reached. Then add four drops of crocodile semen, and pass the mixture through a filter. Gather up the resultant liquid and apply to the genitalia, and immediately the application will effect marvels.*"

Since crocodiles are rare in Europe, the semen of certain dogs may be substituted. It is said that Cleopatra believed in this substitution, since dogs were able to avoid extermination by the crocodiles on the banks of the Nile.

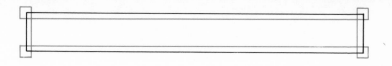

In any case, this experiment, says the tradition, has always been successful, whether crocodiles or dogs are used.

MENS SANA

The ancients realized that physical and psychical conditions are interrelated. Thus Juvenal, the Roman satirist, epitomized this view in his now proverbial phrase, "A healthy mind in a healthy body."

Such a condition, however indirectly, is conducive to amatory proclivities.

MIDDLE AGES

In the Middle Ages, as a result of commercial traffic between the continent of Europe and the East, the Crusades and other wars, travelers' tales, knowledge of philtres, aphrodisiacs, and other sexual stimulants spread from the Arabs and the Moors, from Egypt and India into the European herbals, pharmacopeias, and apothecaries' lore, and, on a more indeterminate level, among alchemists, wizards, and occultists.

Philtres in particular were in great demand. Their ingredients were miscellaneous, sometimes repulsive, but all the more credited with effective results in promoting sexual practices and consummations.

MILK BATHS

Among the Arabs, washing the genitals with asses' milk was considered a means of stimulating vigor.

Poppaea, wife of the Roman Empire Nero, is said to have bathed in asses' milk, for beautifying purposes.

MIMNERUS

This seventh century B.C. poet of Colophon was the first Greek lyric poet to hymn the sexual pleasures of men and women.

MINERAL WATERS

Bathing in certain mineral waters has been an aphrodisiac device for centuries. The procedure was similar to the ancient Romans, who constantly practiced it in resorts throughout the Roman Empire.

In Arabic manuals dedicated to erotic counsel, recommendations are given for such bathing to all who are intent on maintaining or increasing sexual vigor.

Radioactive baths are said to act favorably in a sexual direction. So, too, with arsenical springs, cold water treatment, and hydrotherapy.

The continuing popularity of hot tubs and spas attests to what seems to be an eternal belief in the power of water to effect renewal.

MINT

An aromatic plant used in flavoring foods. Reputed to have aphrodisiac properties, especially by the Hindus who believed it could stimulate the lower chakras, particularly of men.

MISTRESS-GODDESS

King Ptolemy II of the third century built a temple, according to the Greek biographer Plutarch, dedicated to his mistress Belestiche whom he renamed Aphrodite Belestiche.

MIXED DRINKS

Cognac, with the addition of a little paprika and the yolk of an egg, is considered an effective aphrodisiac aid.

MOH

The Moh tree, botanically named Bassia Latifolia, produces flowers rich in sugar and is used in India in the manufacture of the liquor arak.

The *Ananga-Ranga*, the Hindu compendium of sexology, recommends this recipe for the restoration of virility: "The pith of the Moh tree pounded and mixed with cow's milk is taken as a wholesome drink...."

MOLLUSCA

The mollusca, and testaceous animals in particular, have been considered to be of potency in an amatory sense.

MOLY

A legendary plant, with white flowers and black root, endowed with magic virtues. In Homer, Hermes gives the herb to Ulysses to protect him against the wiles of Circe. Usually identified with Allium moly, wild garlic. John Milton mentions the plant moly in *Paradise Lost*.

Although it is not definitively identifiable, moly may well be a Phoenician term, or an Egyptian one used in Greek in a generic sense. It has also been suggested that moly may be equated with wild rue, a plant indigenous to Southern Europe and Asia Minor.

MOST POPULAR APHRODISIAC

Among the ancient Greeks, onions are most frequently mentioned as a stimulus to sexual desire.

MUGWORT

In the Orient, this plant was associated with sexual matters.

MULLER, JOHANNES

Author of a doctoral dissertation entitled *De Febre Amatoria*, published in 1689. He discusses in particular sexual conditions relating to women. Hellebore, he asserts, is a decided anti-aphrodisiac. As aphrodisiac aids he recommends rich banquets that create a sense of euphoria and thus indirectly stimulate amatory inclinations. In regard to drinking, he recommends moderation. In this connection he quotes a short poem of a certain Henry Stephan:

> *I pour out three goblets for wise men.*
> *One for health, that they will first drink.*
> *Then, one for love and pleasure.*
> *The third drink for sleep.*
> *Those who drink the last goblet and*
> *have a reputation for sagacity will*
> *straightaway return to their own homes.*

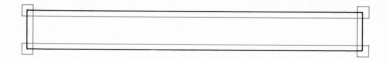

MUSHROOMS

Arabs consider the eating of mushrooms a direct enhancement of the aphrodisiac type.

MUSHROOM SOUP MARIE ANTOINETTE

1/4 cup diced onion
1/2 cup of water
8 thinly sliced mushrooms
1 finely crushed, small garlic clove
1/2 cup dry white wine
1/4 tsp salt

1/8 cup chopped chives
1/4 tsp. dill
1/4 tsp. dried basil
1 Tbsp. olive oil
1 Tbsp. red wine vinegar
1 bay leaf
dash of freshly ground pepper

Pour 1/2 cup of water into a sauce pan and stir in the mushrooms, onions, garlic, bay leaf, salt, wine and pepper. Bring ingredients to a boil and lower the heat. Cover the sauce pan and let the ingredients simmer for 12-15 minutes. Remove from the heat and add basil, dill, olive oil, red wine vinegar and chives. Mix well and chill for at least 2 hours. Garnish with lemon rounds and croutons.

MUSICAL STIMULUS

According to an erotic manual long in use in India, a man who wishes to successfully woo a woman should play on a reed pipe. The pipe is to be dressed with the juice of various plants with aphrodisiac properties.

This belief is not restricted to India. The serenade and the love song have been part of our culture since Eleanor of Aquitaine invented the Courts of Love in the twelfth century.

MUSK

A brown, bitter, volatile substance extracted from a gland near the genitals of the musk-deer and of a species of goat indigenous to Central Asia. In Persia and Tibet musk is used in food for its erotic properties. An Arab writer comments on the efficacy of perfuming oneself with musk as an aid before engaging in sexual activity. According to the *Kama Sutra*, the odor of musk is associated with the ideal woman. It often appears in stories from China as an enticing erotic factor.

An old medical record relates that by means of musk the genital power of a man in his eightieth year was resuscitated.

MUSTARD BATHS

Hot mustard baths have been recommended as assisting the libido in women.

MUSTARD SEED

A strong infusion of mustard seed was formerly believed to be an effective erotic stimulant.

MUTTON

Among Arabs, mutton eaten with caraway seed is thought to be an aphrodisiac.

MYROPOLIA

Myropolia is the name given to perfume shops during Roman times. The perfumes were generally intended as enhancements for sexual purposes and included ingredients imported from every corner of the Roman empire and even beyond—from Spain, India, Egypt and the Northern frontiers. These perfumeries were also used as places of assignation and sexual rendezvous.

MYRRH

A compound of eggs boiled with myrrh, pepper, and cinnamon, taken on several successive days, is recommended by Arabs for strengthening amorous vigor. (see PERFUMES)

This gum is especially prized in the Orient, used as a medicinal aid as well as an erotic stimulant.

MYRTLE

In the Middle Ages pulverized myrtle leaves were applied to the body as a sexual stimulation.

A putative love tonic was made from the water in which myrtle leaves and flowers had been steeped. Used in many European countries. An old recipe advises:

> *The flowers and leaves of myrtle, two hands-fuls, infuse them in two quarts of spring water, and a quart of white wine, for twenty-four hours, and then distil them in a cold still and this will be of a strong scent and tincture, and by adding more or less of the myrtle you may make it stronger or weaker as you please. This beautifies, and mixed with cordial syrups is a good cordial and inclines those that drink it to be very amorous.*

NAPLES

In the kingdom of Naples, during festival time in the town of Trani, a gigantic wooden statue of the ancient god Priapus was carried in the procession. The prominent phallus of this effigy was affectionately called *Il Santo Membro*, or the Holy Member.

The ancient ceremony was evidently a relic of antiquity, a celebration in honor of Bacchus, the father of Priapus. It continued until the beginning of the eighteenth century, when it was finally abolished by ecclesiastical authority.

NATURAL PHILOSOPHY

Next to mathematics, the study of natural philosophy tends to have anti-aphrodisiac effects. One erotologist adds, "requiring, as it does, the unremitting attention of the student, his perambulation of the open country, and the personal observation of all animated objects."

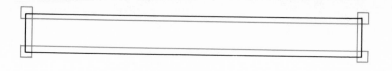

NEFZAWI

Umar ibn Muhammed al-Nefzawi, the author of *The Perfumed Garden*, lived in Southern Tunisia. Here he produced his remarkable erotic manual. The preface says that "the author was animated by the most praiseworthy intentions."

The Introduction itself warns that the work is not to be considered as a lascivious or obscene text, but is highly motivated, for the Sheik begins: "Praise be given to God, who has placed man's greatest pleasure in the genitalia of women and has destined the *partes genitales* of man to afford the greatest enjoyment to women."

The subjects of the manual range from sexual physiology to conception. A chapter is devoted to men who are held in contempt. Another treats of women who deserve to be praised. Medicines, aphrodisiacs, and sexual rites are discussed with great precision and lucidity.

NEPENTHES

A drug or potion frequently mentioned by Homer, especially in the *Odyssey*, as having the effect of banishing sorrow or mental trouble. It has been variously identified with opium, hashish, and particularly the *Panax Chironium* of Theophrastus, the third century B.C. Greek philosopher who wrote on plants.

Theophrastus asserts that, infused in wine, this drug was administered as an aphrodisiac.

NEWTON

It is recorded that Sir Isaac Newton, the famous mathematician, is reputed to have lived without ever having had sexual intimacy. (see MATHEMATICS)

NICOTINE

The nicotine in tobacco has been held to produce anti-aphrodisiac effects in men due to the reduction in blood flow to the genital region.

NINJIN

A root highly regarded by the Japanese. It has properties that putatively are analogous to the aphrodisiac virtues of the mandrake. (see MANDRAKE)

NUOC-MAN

An aphrodisiac sauce, consisting of extract of decayed fish, much in use in the Far East, especially among the Chinese. It contains the two basic aphrodisiac elements, phosphorous and salt. The sauce is often spiced with pimento and garlic.

NUTMEG

An aromatic seed of a tree native to the East Indies. Used to spice food. Highly prized in the Orient as an aphrodisiac, especially among women. The dose necessary for intoxication is far in excess of amounts normally used in cooking and can be toxic.

NUTRITION

Experiments have demonstrated that sexual interest and sexual desire increase with nutritional satisfaction, and that inversely a lowering of nutritional diet coincides with a diminution of sexual expression. As a general rule, therefore, any kind of faulty nutrition will affect sexual ability. The importance of proper diet is emphasized or implicit in all manuals of erotology, both European and Oriental. For continued virility, a balanced diet would consist of the consumption of adequate quantities of fats, minerals, carbohydrates, and proteins.

NYMPHAEA

A Hindu aphrodisiac, in the form of a compound applied to the body, is oil of hogweed, echites putescens, the sarina plant, yellow amaranth, and the leaf of the nymphaea.

NYMPHS

In Greek mythology, the female counterparts to the satyrs. Roaming the forests and streams, these delectable provocateurs of passion without constraint would search out youths to favor with their embraces and otherwise frolic with their satyr companions.

OCTOPUS

The sepia octopus was once in great repute as an aphrodisiac. In *Casina*, by the Roman comedy writer Plautus, there is a scene in which an old man has just been purchasing some at the fish market.

OLIBANUM

Olibanum is the biblical frankincense. An aromatic resin once used in medicine and now used as incense.

It was known to Greeks and Romans and many other ancient peoples and was prized as a perfume during the Middle Ages.

The Arabs compounded it with honey and nutmeg for use as a sexual specific. The Turks combined olibanum with myrrh, camphor, and musk in a pulverized form. The resultant perfume was said to invigorate the genitals.

ONIONS

Onions and similar bulbous plants have a legendary reputation for aphrodisiac qualities. The Roman poet Ovid, in his *Remedy for Love*, recommends the onion. Martial, the Roman epigrammatist, advises, "If your wife is old and your member is exhausted, eat onions in plenty."

In the case of men, onions add virility; in women, they purify the blood.

Oriental dishes intended as aphrodisiacs frequently contain onions. A popular dish among Arabs is a compound of onions and egg yolks.

An old European recipe that was reputed to have been a potent aphrodisiac consisted of cooked onions in a salad, mixed with oil, pepper, salt, and vinegar.

ONION SEED

In *The Perfumed Garden*, Nefzawi suggests a stimulant: Pound onion seed, sift it, mix it with honey. Stir the mixture well. Take this concoction while fasting.

Another Arab dish recommended for sexual potency is onions boiled with condiments and aromatic spices, then fried in oil and yolk of eggs. The preparation is to be taken on several successive days.

A writer of ancient Greek comedy says: "Onions are hard to digest, though nourishing and strengthening to the stomach: they are cleansing but they weaken the eyesight, and they also stimulate sexual desire."

According to the Greek physician Galen, pounded onion seed, mixed with honey and taken while undergoing fasting, has aphrodisiac qualities.

ORCHID

Etymologically, this name signifies "testes" in Greek. This plant, whose shape has more than symbolic similarity to the male genitalia, has had an unwarranted reputation as an aphrodisiac.

However, these visually intoxicating flowers, particularly the lady slipper orchid, are potent stimulants to the eye and the imagination. The gift of a lady slipper orchid gets the point across in a beautiful way.

ORGANOTHERAPY

Popular as a treatment for sexual disorders from at least Roman times and up until the middle of the twentieth century, this treatment consisted of the consumption of animal genitalia—stags, roosters, asses, and even monkeys—as a means of recovering sexual potency. The testes of animals were also used for this purpose and meals were compounded largely with these ingredients.

ORTHAON

The name of one of the twelve mythological creatures known as centaurs. A centaur was part human, part equine, and was associated with a cult on Mount Helicon. Orthaon means erection.

OSPHRESIOLOGY

The study of aromas and olfactory reactions. In a special anthropological sense, the study concerns the various human scents and their connection to sexual activity.

Other aromas—vegetable scents and animal odors—have been enlisted for amatory stimulus through the sense of smell with profound sexual repercussions.

The act of mutual smelling or sniffing is itself an aphrodisiac procedure. An example is the Chittagong tribe whose lovers inhale each other's odor as a stimulus to romance rather than kiss.

OVID

In his *Ars Amatoria*, or The Art of Love, the Roman poet describes a number of items that were associated in Roman times, sometimes wrongly, with aphrodisiac properties:

> *Some teach that herbs will efficacious prove,*
> *But in my judgement such things poison love.*
> *Pepper with biting nettle-seed they bruise,*
> *With yellow pellitory wine infuse.*
> *Venus with such as this no love compels,*
> *Who on the shady hill of Erys dwells.*
> *Eat the white shallots sent from Megara*
> *Or garden herbs that aphrodisiac are,*
> *Or eggs, or honey on Hymettus flowing,*
> *Or nuts upon the sharp-leaved pine trees*
> *growing.*

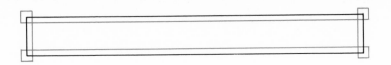

He further condemns aphrodisiac aids such as hippomanes, magic herbs, exorcism formulas, and love philtres. In his opinion, they had no effectiveness since even the enchantresses Circe and Medea could not, by their black arts, prevent the infidelity of Odysseus and Jason.

OYSTERS

The oyster does not seem to deserve its age-old reputation as an aphrodisiac. In all probability, the association of oysters with sexuality derives from the fact that, on the half shell, they are said to resemble the female genitalia.

Nevertheless, oysters have remained a stable ingredient in our fantasies of pleasure. (Remember the famous eating scene in that ode to sensual excess, *Tom Jones*?)

PADMINI

The Lotus-Woman. In Hindu erotic literature, the ideal woman. Gifted physically and emotionally with all the perfect characteristics of Oriental feminine seductiveness.

PAMPHILA

A Roman matron of the first century A.D., who wrote a little monograph, no longer extant, entitled *On Sexual Enjoyments*.

PAN

A Greek god of the mountains and forests whose most dominant characteristic is continuous lustfulness. His goat feet are associated with the goat itself, whose characteristic is a vast amorous propensity.

The attendants of Pan are satyrs, equally characterized by lustful inclinations. The Greek expression *pan* signifies "everything," and the implication is that the entire cosmos is permeated and conditioned by the procreative force.

PAPRIKA

Hungarian red pepper. It is compounded from the plant *Capsicum annum* and is credited with being a powerful aphrodisiac.

PASTRY

Honey, ginger, syrup of vinegar, pellitory, cardamoms, cinnamon, garlic, long pepper, nutmeg, hellebore, and Chinese cinnamon, compounded into a cake are a specific Arab prescription for potency.

In the Middle Ages in particular aphrodisiacs were commonly kneaded into breads and pastries intended for particular persons or used in intimate banquets. (see APHRODISIAC CAKES)

PEACHES

Among the fruits considered rich in aphrodisiac properties.

PEAS

One of the interesting things about aphrodisiacs is that so many of them are so common to our diet. This pea dish was recommended by the author of *The Perfumed Garden* as one that creates passion: Green peas boiled with onions, powdered with cinnamon, ginger and cardamoms well pounded. (see PERFUMED GARDEN)

PEPPER

Used as a condiment. Compounded with nettle-seed,
it was credited with exciting sexual impulses. Both
white and red pepper are considered to have this
property.

PERCH

In the head of this fish there are supposedly small
stones that sorceresses used in concocting
love-philtres.

PERFUMED BEDS

Perfume as a stimulus to sexual arousal is mentioned
in the Bible in connection with the adulterous woman:

> *I have perfumed my bed with myrrh, aloes,*
> *and cinnamon.*
> *Come, let us take our fill of love until the*
> *morning,*
> *let us solace ourselves with love.*

Perhaps Dr. Graham read this in preparation for the
construction of his Celestial Bed. (see GRAHAM)

PERFUMED GARDEN

A manual of Arabian erotic technique, written in the
sixteenth century by Sheik al-Nefwazi. It was translated into French in the nineteenth century. Sir
Richard Burton, the noted Orientalist, translated it
into English.

PERFUMED GENITALIA

From the earliest times in Egypt, in Hellenistic Alexandria, in eighteenth century France, and in some parts of Europe and the Orient to this day, women have had a practice of using small perfumed pads. The intention was to arouse the utmost sensory excitation in their lovers. The perfumed sacs were inserted into the woman's body before sexual activity.

PERFUMES

Among the Romans in particular, erotic impulses were encouraged by the lavish use of exotic perfumes and unguents. Perfumes were used on the body, on the head and hair, and on garments. Civet and ambergris were especially popular among the wealthy, leisurely, sophisticated set. Aromatic spices, too, were an aid to sweetened breath. *Foliatum* was an ointment prepared from spikenard. Another perfume was known as *nicerotiana*, named after its originator Nicerotas. Myrrh, cinnamon, sweet marjoram, and the plumlike myrobalan fruit were likewise usual ingredients of aromatic preparations.

Arab erotic manuals stress the importance of perfumes, for both men and women, as an indirect and subtle stimulant in amorous techniques.

Mohammed mentions his love of women and perfumes. Biographers write of men who gave out an enticing personal fragrance from their bodies. Plutarch, for instance, the Greek biographer, says that

the body of Alexander the Great gave off a scent of violets. Goethe calls such men "human flowers."

Among primitive races and Orientals the olfactory kiss is believed to produce a powerful sexual reaction.

In his play *Volpone*, Ben Jonson has Volpone make this amatory offer to Celia:

> *Thy baths shall be the juice of July-flowers,*
> *Spirit of roses, and of violets,*
> *The milk of unicorns, and panthers' breath*
> *Gathered in bags, and mixed with Cretan*
> *wines.*
> *Our drink shall be prepared gold and amber;*
> *Which we will take, until my roof whirl round*
> *With the vertigo.*

Perfumed oils have been part of the romantic ritual since our beginnings. Lady Sara Cunningham has classified all the scents related to sexual response according to the planetary rulers of astrology. Here are just a few of those connected to Venus: almond oil, aloe-wood oil, bigonia oil, birch oil, camellia oil, coriander oil, hawthorn oil, rose oil, and vanilla oil.

PERSIAN RECIPE

Put cloves, cinnamon, and cardamoms in a jar with rose water and steep your husband's shirt in it with a piece of parchment inscribed with his name and the names of four angels. Heat together over a fire. When the mixture boils, the husband's love will increase.

PERSPIRATION

Often acts as a powerful stimulant to the male. Henry III of Navarre and Henry IV are said to have inadvertantly inspired a passion in Maria of Cleves and Gabrielle respectively through the transmission of a handkerchief used to wipe away perspiration.

PERSUASIVE METHOD

Erotic intimacy, as all the love manuals warn—Hindu, Arab, Chinese, and Roman—should be preceded by enticing amorous preludes. In the words of Ovid, the great Roman poet: "Believe me, the pleasures of love must not be hastened, but should be allured forth gently with lingering delay."

PETIT SOUPER

A Little Supper. A French custom, popular in the eighteenth century, that, by its intimacy and the offering of specially prepared heartening dishes, was a decided factor in increasing erotic sensibility among the few, selected guests. Such instances of the marriage of love and gastronomy were frequent.

PETRARCH

Fourteenth century Italian poet and humanist. Of love, he said that it is a hidden fire, a pleasing wound, a palatable poison, a bitter sweetness, a delightful sickness, a joyous torture, an indulgent death.

PHALLIC SYMBOLS

The term phallus is reputedly of Phoenician origin. In Sanskrit it is the root that means "to burst forth," "to

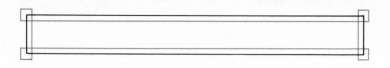

be fruitful." *Phal* itself also means "ploughshare."

In biblical literature the root occurs in Genesis 46.9 with the mention of Phallu. Phallu is believed to signify "the distinguished one," "the one who divides," a reference to sensual love.

Such symbols, dedicated to the cosmic procreative force, appeared in the temple at Heliopolis in Syria, and in the shrines of Thebes in Egypt. The temple at Karnak was also adorned with phallic reliefs.

PHEASANT

Like most game, it is associated with fertility and virility, and is considered highly aphrodisiac in effect.

PHERAMONES

Contemporary scientists are experimenting with human odors related to sex in the form of pheramones, which may be our language of courtship on a very subtle but powerful olfactory level. The word "pheramone," coined by scientists in 1959, means "to transfer excitement." There is as yet no conclusive proof of the effect of pheramones on sexual arousal.

PHILTRE

A magic potion usually intended to induce amorous effects on the drinker. The ancient Greeks and Romans were familiar with the aphrodisiac purposes of such drinks. In his *Marriage Precepts*, for instance, the historian Plutarch mentions them specifically. Exotic or repulsive ingredients generally formed the

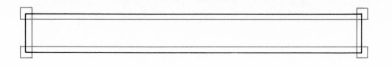

base of the potions and included briony, mandrake root, tobacco, the bones of frogs, betel nuts, sparrow liver, the genitals, entrails, testes of hare, hare kidney, fingers, human and animal excrement, blood and brains of sparrow, semen of stag, animal secretions, as well as flesh, brain, urine, ambergris, roast heart of humming bird, powdered. Shakespeare's *Macbeth* contains the famous scene depicting three witches concocting such a potion.

Love philtres have continuously been a folk means of inspiring passion. Many European legends and sagas of various types, together with ballads and popular beliefs, emphasize the erotic powers of such potions. The administration of such philtres still prevails in outlying areas, in secluded valleys, and agricultural districts throughout the European continent.

The Romans dwell frequently and with descriptive detail on philtres. Horace speaks of potions to excite desire as if they were a matter of common knowledge. The poet Propertius refers to a philtre containing snake bones, a toad, and the feathers of a screech-owl. Apuleius, the novelist, in his *Metamorphoses*, includes among such ingredients a skull torn from between the teeth of a wild beast.

Perhaps one of the most famous aphrodisiacs of all is the one described in Shakespeare's *Midsummer Night's Dream*, the chief ingredient of which is the pansy:

Oberon, *That very time I saw, but thou couldst not*
Flying between the cold moon and the earth,
Cupid all arm'd, a certain aim he took
At a fair vestal throned by the west,
And loos'd his love-shaft smartly from his bow,
As it should pierce a hundred thousand hearts;
But I might see young Cupid's fiery shaft
Quench'd in the chaste beams of the wat'ry moon,
And the imperial votaress passed on,
In maiden meditation, fancy-free.
Yet mark'd I where the bolt of Cupid fell.
It fell upon a little western flower.

Before milk-white, now purple with love's wound,
And maidens call it Love-in-Idleness.
Fetch me that flower; the herb I show'd thee once,
The juice of it on sleeping eyelids laid
Will make or man or woman madly dote
Upon the next live creature that it see.
Fetch me this herb; and be thou here again
Ere the leviathan can swim a league.

Puck, *I'll put a girdle round about the earth*
In forty minutes.

Oberon, *Having once this juice,*

I'll watch Titania when she is asleep,
And drop the liquor of it in her eyes,
The next thing then she waking looks upon,
Be it on lion, bear, or wolf, or bull,
On meddling monkey, or on busy ape,
She shall pursue it with the soul of love,
And ere I take this charm off from her sight,
As I can take it with another herb,
I'll make her render up her page to me.

In the Middle Ages, when witchcraft and thaumaturgic practices were rampant over Europe, sorceresses did a roaring trade in magic brews designed to excite passion or to preserve affection. These witches became primary and valuable consultants in these amatory challenges.

It happened that some philtres were effective, but a great many, concocted not only of repellent but poisonous ingredients led to disastrous results. Yet the demand for any means to attain sexual mastery was so intense, so continuous, so widespread, among princelings and peasants, serf and squire, kings and burghers, that peripatetic vendors, proclaiming with effrontery and assurance the efficacy of secret potions in their possession and oral recipes, reaped rich harvests throughout the European countries.

PHOSPHORUS

Foods containing this element are considered to be aphrodisiac in effect. However, phosphorus taken in doses large enough to cause stimulation is poisonous.

PHYLAX

An ancient farcical performance with actors wearing false erections and replete with obscenity. The phylax was popular in southern Italy. It was accompanied by music and indecent dances with a large helping of transvestism—all intended to arouse sexual feelings in the audience.

PIMENTO

Now used as a spice. In 1132, however, Peter the Venerable forbade the monks of Cluny to use it because of its aphrodisiac properties.

When pimento and pepper are boiled together with a species of mallow, the resultant compound is applied to riceflour poultices, which in turn are placed in contact with the male genitals. This is a Chinese prescription that is highly hazardous, but is used externally as a stimulant.

PINE SEEDS

In the East, greatly prized as a strong aphrodisiac.

PISTACHIO

Pistaci vera. A nut frequently mentioned in Arab erotic manuals for its aphrodisiac value.

PLAICE

Another fish of reputedly aphrodisiac value.

PLOVER'S EGGS

Stuffed with various spices, this dish, called Plover's

Eggs à la Du Barry, has the reputation of being irres-
istible to amorous assaults.

POETIC ADVICE

Nefzawi, discussing amatory excesses in *The Perfumed Garden*, adds:

> *Having thus treated of the dangers which may
> occur from the coitus, I have considered it
> useful to bring to your knowledge the follow-
> ing verses, which contain hygienic advice in
> their respect. These verses have been com-
> posed by the order of Haroun e Rachid by the
> most celebrated physician of his time, whom
> he had asked to inform him of the remedies
> for successfully combating the ills caused by
> coition.*

> *Eat slowly, if your food shall do you good,
> and take good care, that it be well digested.
> Beware of things which want hard mastica-
> tion. They are bad nourishment, so keep from
> them. Drink not directly after finishing your
> meal, or else you go half way to meet an
> illness. Keep not within you what is of excess.
> And if you were in most susceptible circles,
> attend to this well before seeking your bed,
> for rest this is the first necessity. From drugs
> and medicine keep well away, and do not use
> them unless very ill. Use all precautions
> proper, for they keep your body sound, and
> are the best support. Don't be too eager for*

round-breasted women. Excess of pleasure
soon will make you feeble, and in coition you
will find a sickness. And before all beware of
aged women, for their embraces will to you be
poison. Each second day a bath should wash
you clean; Remember these precepts and fol-
low them.

POMEGRANATE

According to Pliny the Elder, the Roman encyclopedist, the pith of the pomegranate tree was conducive
to sexual activity. The fruit of the pomegranate is
known in many cultures as a symbol for fertility.

POTATO

Although the potato actually has no exciting value, it
was believed in the seventeenth century to possess
aphrodisiac qualities and is frequently mentioned in
this respect in Elizabethan drama. Its effectiveness
was supposedly related to that of the eryngo or sea
holly root. Shakespeare referred to it in *The Merry
Wives of Windsor*:

Let the sky rain potatoes,
kissing comfits and snow eryngoes.

(Act V, Scene 5)

POTIONS

Love potions, though effective, could also be highly
dangerous and actually lead to death. In both ancient
and medieval times such potions were often administered to lovesick girls, women, elders, and others

whose libido required stimulus.

St. Jerome, for instance, relates that the Roman poet Lucretius was poisoned by a love philtre.

On occasion, the potion was believed to affect the mind. In his *Remedium Amoris*, an erotic poetic manual, the poet Ovid says,

> *Philtres that cause pallor of the complexion*
> *are worthless for young women. They disturb*
> *the balance of the mind and light the fires of*
> *frenzied madness.*

But the urge for sexual activity was often so desperate that the potential and frequently actual hazards associated with potions were completely disregarded.

Lucullus, the Roman general who flourished in the first century B.C., and who was also a famous gourmet, was rendered unconscious, according to the Greek biographer Plutarch and the Roman Cornelius Nepos, by drinking love potions.

It was also said that the Roman Emperor Caligula was thrown into a fit by a potion given him by his wife Caesonia. She had intended the drink as a stimulating aphrodisiac.

The administration of love potions in Rome became so involved in criminal acts that imperial decrees periodically made the giving of a love potion a punishable offense, occasionally, even subject to the capital penalty.

PRAWNS

The aphrodisiac nature of prawns is evident in an epigram by the Greek poet Asclepiades:

For a meal with a courtesan a purchase is to be made at the market of three large and ten small fish and twenty-four prawns.

PRIAPUS

In ancient mythology, Priapus is the divinity whose symbol is the phallus. He is the son of Dionysus and Aphrodite and represents the elemental physical principle of Eros. The goose, reputed to possess high generative power, was sacred to Priapus.

On coins from Lampsacus, a city on the Hellespont, he is shown with an erection.

In Roman times, his cult was celebrated in special shrines, in rural communities, and among fishermen and sailors.

Priapus was frequently represented sculpturally as a kind of scarecrow and even as a protection in graveyards.

In medieval towns there were still devotees who paid homage to the antique god Priapus. They came as suppliants suffering from maladies associated with the god's attributes. Images were offered to the deity, as well as reproductions of the genital parts that were affected. These offerings were in the form of paintings or figurines fashioned from wax, wood, or marble. Women made offerings of flowers. Priapus was the

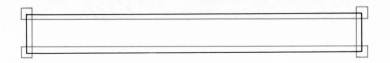

tutelary deity of the city of Antwerp until the sixteenth century.

PULLEIAR

The Hindu erotic double symbol representing the lingam and the yoni, the Hindu words for the male and female genitalia. The pulleiar was venerated by the worshippers of Siva, one of the triune deities of India.

PYRETHRUM

Pyrethrum is a kind of chrsanthemum. In ancient times it was used medicinally and known as pellitory.

The Arabs used an ointment compounded of pyrethrum, ginger, and lilac ointment as a genital stimulant.

QUINCE

Reputedly, jelly made from the quince has a decidedly
erotic effect.

QUININE

Taken in the evening, quinine is considered by the
Persians to be an aphrodisiac aid.

RADISH

Radishes, beans, peas, and lentils were once popular in Germany as aids to virility.

Radishes in particular were held in such high esteem as to warrant a poem. Entitled *Raporum Encomium*—Eulogy of Radishes—this glorification was published in Latin in 1540 at Lyons. The author was Claude Bigothier.

The Egyptians of the fifth century B.C. commonly used a concoction made of radishes mixed with honey for aphrodisiac purposes.

RAKTA-BOL

The Hindu name for myrrh. Powdered rakta-bol was used as an ointment when mixed with *costus arabicus*, manishil, borax, and aniseed.

RAWILOID

Also known as reserpine or snake root. A drug used to reduce high blood pressure. It is often confused with aristolochia, also called snake root.

The drug is extracted from the dried root of *rauwolfia serpentina*. This plant has been used in India for thousands of years for all kinds of illness, commonly as a headache remedy. In Sanskrit the plant is known as sarpagandha, which signifies "insanity cure."

The active principle, rauwolfia, is extracted from the powdered roots of the plant. The dried root was chewed by holy men of India as an aid to contemplation. Mahatma Gandhi used it regularly.

The plant also grows in the Phillipines, China, Java, and South America. It has a depressive effect on some people.

REPTILES

The Romans used many kinds of reptiles in aphrodisiac preparations.

RESIN

All kinds of resins were used by the ancient Greeks and Roman as aphrodisiac ingredients.

RICE

According to Hindu erotology, an effective sexual prescription runs as follows. "A drink made from sparrows' eggs and rice, boiled in milk, to which are added honey and ghee."

The Hindu *Ars Amatoria*, the *Ananga-Ranga*, gives this prescription for erotic potency: Wild rice mixed with honey of equal weight, eaten in the evening.

In Britain, too, rice is reputed to increase the sexual faculties.

RICE OIL

This yellowish oil is obtained from the fresh leaves of a plant called *ruta graveolens*. Its effect is similar to that of cantharides, or Spanish fly, but somewhat milder in action.

ROCKET

A species of cabbage that grows in the Mediterranean region, used in salads. Reputed to be an aphrodisiac. Mentioned by the Roman Poet Horace in this connection. Martial, too, the Roman epigrammatist, refers to it along with other aphrodisiacs:

> *Scallions, lustful rockets nought prevail,*
> *And heightening meats in operation fail;*
> *Thy wealth begins the pure cheeks to defile,*
>
> *So venery provoked lives but a while;*
> *Who can admire enough, the wonder's such,*
> *That thy not standing stands thee in so much?*

Rocket, which is *brasica eruca*, possessed, according to the ancients, the virtue of restoring vigor to the genitalia. Hence it was consecrated to Priapus, and also sown around the sites of his statues.

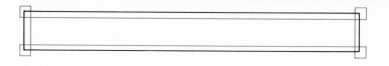

In this regard, Columella, the Roman bucolic poet, says:

Th'eruca, Priapus, near thee we sow
To rouse to duty husbands who are slow.

Seasoned with olive oil, vinegar, pepper, and chopped garlic, rocket salad was touted by Ovid and others as a fine aphrodisiac.

ROE

Cod and herring roe are considered high in aphrodisiac potential.

ROMAN APHRODISIACS

A list of such items appears in the poet Ovid's *Ars Amatoria*, Book 2:

There are some who advise taking the noxious herb savory; in my judgment it is poison. Or they mix pepper with the seed of prickly nettle and yellow pellitory pounded in old wine. But the goddess whom lofty Eryx holds on his shady mount does not let herself thus be forced to her joys. Let white onions be taken, that are sent from the Pelasgian city of Alcathous, and the salacious herb that comes from the garden (rocket), and eggs, and Hymettian honey, and the nuts that the sharp-leaved pine brings forth.

ROMAN ENTICEMENTS

To increase amatory advances, the Romans fre-

quented baths regularly and often. Pastilles were eaten
to perfume the breath. Oils, pomades, and unguents
were also used, as well as rouge, creams, and preparations for the cheeks, hair, teeth, and nails.

An ancient writer describes the procedures in use:

> *They beautify their skin with an array of cos-*
> *metics...each maid carries something, a silver*
> *jar, a phial, a mirror...to polish the teeth or*
> *blacken the eyebrows and lashes.... The lady*
> *dips her hair in henna to redden it and dries it*
> *in the midday sun.... Another lady thinks*
> *black hair becomes her...with steel tongs she*
> *forces her curls into shape.*

ROOSTER

Brillat-Savarin, the famous French writer on gastronomy, recommends the potency of this dish, an old
rooster, ground beef, parsley, turnips. All cooked
separately, then mixed together and boiled once more.

ROSEMARY

An aromatic shrub indigenous to Southern Europe.
The leaves are used medicinally, in perfumery, and in
cookery. Also known to the Romans, and reputed as
an amatory stimulant.

SAFFLOWER

A thistle-like plant. In the fourth century it was highly recommended as a sexual stimulant.

SAFFRON

According to ancient legend, a Greek girl partaking of saffron for an entire week could not resist a lover. The reputation of saffron as an aphrodisiac has not wholly disappeared, although it is now used largely as a condiment in food.

A concoction consisting of saffron, orange blossoms, dried dates, anise, wild carrots, and egg yolk, boiled in clear water into which honey and the blood of two freshly killed doves have been poured, is recommended by Arabs as a sexual inducement.

SAGE

A plant who aromatic leaves are used for culinary purposes.

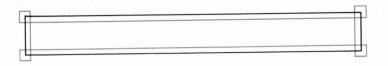

The juice, mixed with honey, is used for strengthening the voice and as a throat gargle. Sage also has a reputed stimulating value.

SALADS

At various times and in different areas salads, compounded of meats, spices, and tubers have been thought to have aphrodisiac value.

Among these are a salad of tulip bulbs, tomato salad—the tomato often being assumed to be a love-apple—salad dressing of vinegar, garlic, and salt.

SALEP

A jelly-like preparation made from the dried root of the *orchis morio*, which is the Turkish satyrion. Used in the Middle East formerly as a drug, also as a food.

In Turkey, Iran, and Syria salep is popular as a restorative and also as a provocative to amatory activity.

SALMON

Reputed to have high aphrodisiac value.

SALVIA

A genus to which the plant sage belongs. Used for garnishing, also of aphrodisiac repute.

SALT

In ancient times and in the Middle Ages, salt was believed to be an aphrodisiac. It was associated with Venus, the Roman goddess of love and her Greek counterpart, Aphrodite, who was said to have risen

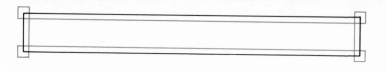

from the sea.

SANDIX CEROPOLIUM

This plant was credited long ago with exciting amorous propensities. Tiberius, the dissolute Roman emperor, is said to have exacted a certain quantity of the herb from the Germanic tribes as tribute.

It was supposedly used in Sweden to encourage husbands in their matrimonial functions.

SATYRION

An obscure, unidentifiable plant, probably similar to the *orchis*. Known to the Greeks and Romans as a powerful aphrodisiac. The plant has smooth red leaves and a double root, the lower part of which is believed to be helpful in conceiving males, the upper part, females. According to some authorities, satyrion is akin to the Iris florantina. Also called Serapias. Serapias has pear-shaped leaves, a tall stem, and a root of two tubers having the appearance of testicles.

The root was dissolved in goat's milk, and the reaction was so potent that, according to the historian Theophrastus, it produced on one occasion seventy consecutive acts of coitus.

Another species of satyrion was called erithraicon. If held in the hand, the plant provoked desire. To make the erotic desire subside, lettuce was eaten.

In ancient mythology, the efficaciousness of satyrion is attested, particularly in the case of Hercules. Pliny the Elder, the Roman encyclopedist, declares that it power to arouse sexual excitement is common knowledge. Petronius, the Roman novelist, also refers to the plant in his *Satyricon*, "We saw in the chambers persons of both sexes, acting in such a way that I concluded they must all have been drinking satyrion."

Again, "So saying, she brought me a goblet full of satyrion and with jests and quips and a host of marvelous tales induced me to drink up nearly all the liquor."

SATYRS

In Greek mythology, spirits of the woods. Half animal, usually in the form of a goat, and half human. They are the attendants of the rustic god Pan. The satyrs are characterized by bestiality and lust, and represent the elemental sexual passions of man.

SAVORY

A perennial used for seasoning. Aromatic and hot-flavored.

Formerly cultivated for its aphrodisiac properties. This herb—satureia—was well known to the ancient Romans in particular.

SEAL OF THE SNAKE

A stone that, according to Moslem lore, was extractd from a snakes's head. It was commonly used as a love charm. (see REPTILES)

SEASONAL INFLUENCES

The seasons of the year, and the temperature, subtly influence amorous desires. Hesiod, an ancient Greek poet, author of *Work and Days*, dwells on the time

> *When the artichoke flowers and the chirping*
> *cicada, perched upon a tree, pours down its*
> *shrill song continuously from beneath its*
> *wings in the season of tiring summer, the kids*
> *are fattest, and wine is most mellow, and the*
> *women are most lustful, but men are feeblest,*
> *for the skin is dry through the heat.*

SEA-SLUG

Found commonly on Western Indian islands. Known widely for its efficacious aphrodisiac virtues. Among the fishermen of Naples, it is called "sea Priapus."

SECRET RITES

Since sexual activity was primarily associated with procreation, and procreation was the basis of a society's continued existence, rites and mystic knowledge involving sexual matters and methods of stimulating amatory tendencies were vested in small, specialized, secretive agencies, notably priests and sorcerers. This was especially true in ancient Egypt, Greece, and Rome.

SENSE OF SMELL

From various sources, both ancient and modern, bodily exhalations and contrived perfumes produce marked impacts on the erotic inclinations.

An early authority asserts:

Odors act powerfully upon the nervous system, they prepare it for all the pleasurable sensations, they communicate to it that slight disturbance of commotion which appears as if inseparable from emotions of delight, all which may be accounted for by their exercising a special action upon those organs whence originated the most rapturous pleasure of which our nature is susceptible.

SESAME

In Hindu erotology a sexual stimulant is made as follows: The outer covering of sesame seeds, steeped in sparrows' eggs and boiled in milk, ghee, and sugar, also the fruits of the kasurika plant and the trapa bispinosa. Beans and flour of wheat are then added. The concoction forms a drink.

SEVENTEENTH CENTURY APHRODISIACS

In his *Tableau de l'Amour Conjugal*, Dr. Nicolas Venette, a French physician, discusses as aphrodisiac items common in his time: cocks' testes, milk, sweet wine, yolk of eggs, prawns, crayfish, beef marrow, garlic, artichokes, hippomanes, campion.

SEXUAL DEITIES

Among the ancient Romans, sex consciousness was so intense that beginning with the marriage ceremony each aspect of cohabitation was associated with a different deity.

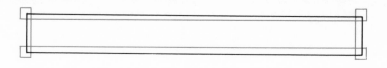

The deities specifically connected to the consummation of a marriage were Prema, Subigus, Juno, and
Pertunda, each of whom has a specific assigned func-
tion in the procedure. The most ancient of all these
Roman deities was Mutunus Tutunus.

SHALLOT

A small onion, used in sauces and salads. The Roman
epigrammatist Martial refers to its aphrodisiac value:
"If envious age relax the nuptial knot, Thy food be
scallions, and thy feast shallot." (see ONIONS)

SHEEP

In Persia, newly married couples were presented with
sheep's hooves steeped in vinegar as a love enticement.

SHELL-FISH

All kinds of shell-fish were considered by the Greeks
as aphrodisiacs. In modern times the same traditional
belief prevails.

SHOWERS

One Arab writer recommends cold showers, twice
daily, and cold compresses as a cure for lack of sexual
vigor.

SHRIMP

Most sea foods, particularly shrimp, are a wide-spread
and traditional enticement for erotic encounters.

SKINK

Latin, *scincus officinalis*. A small lizard, indigenous to

Arabia and North Africa. Formerly prized medicinally. Also once considered, and still treated in Arabia, as a potent aphrodisiac when it is fried in oil.

SNAILS

The ancients considered them as aphrodisiacs. The Roman poets mention them in this respect.

A rejuvenating recipe used in contemporary times requires the following items: Snails boiled with onions, parsley, and garlic, then fried in olive oil. Then boiled again in strong red wine.

SNUFF

According to Sheik Nefzawi, author of *The Perfumed Garden*, snuff, plain or scented, acts as an aphrodisiac.

SOUP

Fish soup, in Hindu erotology, is assumed to have an aphrodisiac value.

Among stimulating soups are onion soup, cheese soup, lentil soup, mushroom soup, celery soup.

SPA

The English spa at Bath was the most fashionable of all and was especially recommended for rejuvenating the passions. Needless to say, license and debauchery entered the lively atmosphere, as well as an array of prostitutes and quacks selling aphrodisiacs and cures for the unpleasant ills resulting from sensual excess.

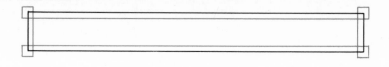

SPANISH FLY

Spanish fly, or cantharides, was known for centuries as a powerful aphrodisiac associated with the subjugation of perhaps unwilling partners. It is a highly toxic substance that often proved lethal to those who used it.

STURGEON SOUP

The sturgeon is considered to be rich in aphrodisiac elements. In the Mediterranean area this is a very popular dish.

SWAN

The swan's magnificient, majestic beauty has been associated with erotic love and surrender from the myth of Leda and Zeus, as the divine swan, to Swan Lake. The aphrodisiac effect of gazing at swans gliding across a misty lake is well-attested by lovers everywhere.

TARRAGON

A plant indigenous to Southeastern Europe. The
aromatic leaves of the plant are used to flavor salads.
Reputed of aphrodisiac value.

TELEPHILON

Theocritus, an ancient Greek poet, says that the leaf
of a flower called *telephilon* was used by the boys of
Crotona as an amatory oracle. A leaf was placed in
the palm of the hand or on the arm, and then struck
sharply. A crackling sound, as a result, portended a
good omen.

Telephilon has been identified as a kind of pepper
tree, or, according to some, as the poppy.

TOMATO

Believed to be an aphrodisiac mostly because of a mistranslation of its name from the Latin *mala oethiopi-cus*. The French translated this as *pomme de mort*, or "apple of death." Its Latin meaning is "apple of the Moors." The English then mistranslated *pomme de mort* as *pomme d'amour*, or "apple of love." Quite a mistake!

Its initial rarity and its vivid red color also added to its brief reputation as an aphrodisiac.

THYME

This fragrant herb has been in use for medicinal purposes, as a flavoring in cookery, and as an erotic stimulus.

TORTOISE

The tortoise, with its characteristic protrusion of the head and neck, was a symbol sacred to Venus. It represented the procreative principle.

TRIPE

A popular dish commonly believed to be a sexual stimulant.

TROUT

Roman matrons, sexually exhausted, were fond of trout caught in a little stream in the Vosges Mountains.

(see FISH)

TRUFFLES

The truffle is an edible fungus, indigenous to Europe. Known to the Romans. Long considered as a sexual

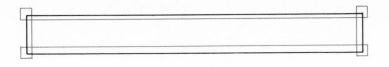

inducement and used for stuffing game, etc. Napoleon was advised by one of his generals to eat truffles to increase potency.

In ancient times, the Romans imported truffles, credited with marked aphrodisiac virtue, from Libya as well as Greece.

Brillat-Savarin, the nineteenth century French gourmet and author of *La Physiologie du Goût*, tells a story in which amatory expression was violently manifested as a result of a dinner that included game and truffles.

TURMERIC

A substance derived from the curcuma, the saffron plant. Considered an effective aphrodisiac stimulant.

TYROLEAN CUSTOM

Among the peasants of the Tyrol, it is customary, during a dancing session, to hold a handkerchief under the armpit; later on, the dancer may give this handkerchief to a reluctant sweetheart, a folk way that is considered effective in inciting amatory responses in the girl.

UNICORN

Sad to say, our image of the magical unicorn—white horse with a single horn—is not the real unicorn. If, indeed, there is one, it is the single horned rhinoceros, whose horn has been valued as a cure-all and an aphrodisiac, especially by the Chinese and the Koreans.

The more familiar unicorn, with its romantic associations of virgins in forests, is worthy as an aphrodisiac only as it stimulates fantasy.

Arab erotic manuals like *The Perfumed Garden* make continual reference to the use of perfume in amatory procedures. The Arabs were the first to develop efficient techniques for extracting essences in order to make the perfumes they deemed necessary to successful lovemaking.

VANILLA

Universally considered a pleasant, aromatic aphrodisiac, although it is often innocuously used in flavoring foods. Its association with sexual activity stems from the fact that the work is a diminutive of the Latin term *vagina*.

Vanilla itself was transplanted from Madagascar, the main source of the spice, to Polynesia a century ago.

Madame de Pompadour was fond of choclates spiced with vanilla and amber.

PERSUASIVE VANILLA PUDDING

4 servings

1/4 cup butter	1/2 cup honey
4 cups milk	2 tsp. vanilla
1/3 cup arrowroot flour	grated lemon rind

Blend the milk, arrowroot flour with the butter, honey and vanilla. Pour the blended mixture into a saucepan.

Bring the blend to a boil, stirring constantly. Simmer another 5 minutes as you continue to stir and then remove the heat. Let cool. Garnish with grated lemon rind.

VANILLA OIL

Used as a base in perfumery. Vanilla itself, *vanilla planifolia*, produces an aromatic substance from the vanilla capsules. Used in flavoring, and once considered, by both gourmets and erotologists, as a powerful amatory stimulant.

VEAL SWEETBREAD

An occasional mention ascribes some sexual virtue to this dish.

VENISON

Medically recommended as a sexual stimulant.

VISUAL APHRODISIAC

A popular dress among ancient Greek women was made of a fine flax that grew on the island of Armorgos, the clothes so fashioned being known as Amorgina. They were thin and transparent, clinging to the contours of the body. Silk fabrics were also favored, particularly those from the island of Cos, and ready-made garments of this material were imported form Assyria.

On one occasion, female flute-players who appeared at a wedding feast were thought by the guests to be completely unclothed, until it was explained that they were wearing Coan dresses.

Later, in Roman times, the novelist Petronius alludes to such dresses as "woven stuff light as air." Seneca, the tutor of the Emperor Nero, a Stoic philosopher and moralist, fulminates against such flimsy, revealing clothes as being erotic encouragements:

I see silken clothes, if those can be called clothes, with which the body or only the private parts could be covered; dressed in them, the woman can hardly swear with a good conscience that she is not naked. These clothes are imported at considerable expense from most distant countries, only that our women may have no more to show their lovers in the bedroom than in the street.

Like perfumes, all such deliberately devised robes made their subtle but distinctive and persistent amatory attack on men.

In museums of Europe, too, there are sculptural representations of the dual god Hermaphroditos in sexual embrace with the god Pan or with the Satyrs. All such visual erotic manifestations tended to add an aphrodisiac stimulus to the beholder.

VISUAL ATTRACTION

Among some primitive tribes, the headdress of girls is capable of arousing sexual desire.

In some cases, photographs, sculptured pieces, shoes, various pieces of female wearing apparel, have potential erotic values in the form of fetishes.

WATER LILY

Related to the lotus, the water lily is also representative of the feminine ideal. Like some other aphrodisiacs, it also has a history of being used for the opposite purpose. Monks and nuns used to drink a concoction of water lilies and poppy syrup to diminish desire.

WEDDING DINNER

Mushrooms, pepper and pine nuts were traditional accompaniments to wedding dinners because of their aphrodisiac properites.

WELLS

In biblical Shittim, immorality was rampant due to the presence of aphrodisiac minerals in the wells which were called the "wells of lewdness." Numbers 25: 1-9.

WHITE WINE

With Juniper berries, a variety of Peruvian bark called *calisaia*, and bitter quassia mixed with bitter orange syrup and white wine taken daily acts as an amatory stimulant.

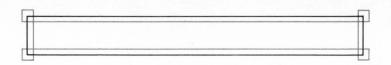

WHITING

Yet another species of fish noted for aphrodisiac value.

WINE

In Biblical literature, in the ancient classics, in the traditional mores of Europe and Asia, wine has uniformly been held in great esteem as a sexual stimulant. From the most remote antiquity to contemporary times wine has been glorified in prose and verse.

A French song runs,

> *To hymn Love, my friends,*
> *You must drink, drink, drink.*

Among the Romans, wine, taken in moderation was considered an effective aphrodisiac. Petronius, in the *Satyricon*, writes:

> *I restricted myself to a moderate use of ungu-*
> *ents. Then, adopting a more fortifying diet,*
> *that is to say onions and snails' heads without*
> *sauce, I also cut down my wine.*

A common beverage credited with aphrodisiac virtue was old wine containing the pungent root of the plant pyrethrum. So too with gentian wine, made from gentian root.

The Roman epigrammatist Martial emphasizes the need for moderation in wine drinking as a requisite for sexual indulgence:

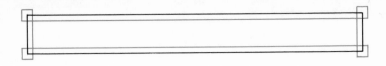

You seldom drink a half measure of watered
Falernian wine, Rufus. Did Naevia promise
you a night of bliss and do you prefer the
assured lubricities of fornication when you are
sober?

Hindu rituals, too, condemn excessive wine drinking
in amatory situations. A drinking rule runs thus:

So long as the steadfast look wavers not,
So long as the mind's light flickers not,
For so long drink! Shun the rest!
Whoso drinks still more is a beast.

In the eighteenth century the wines most in favor
were, burgundy, port, and sherry.

Lucian, the Greek stirist of the second century A.D.,
in describing a festival in Asia, dedicated to Aphrodite, declares:

For more delightful is Aphrodite combined
with Dionysus and both together dispense
more delicious pleasure; but, separate, their
enjoyment is less.... Where the trees stood
thicker and gave more abundant shade, wel-
come seats were placed, whereon people could
take their meals; the townspeople, certainly,
seldom made much use of them, but the great
crowd (of visitors) enjoyed itself there and
there rejoiced in all kinds of love-toying.

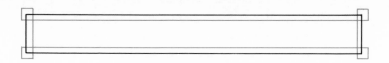

WITCH-HAZEL

Considered at one time as an effective erotic inducement.

WOODCOCK

The woodcock is not only a culinary delight but is reputed to increase seminal fluid.

Vitamin X

Isolated from the leaves of Fo-Ti-Tieng (gotu-kola, or Asian pennywort). Little is known about it. It has been used as an antibiotic.

The leaves of this plant are widely consumed in Ceylon. A French biochemist named Jules Lepine found that it stimulated the endocrine system. Fo-Ti-Tieng means "elixir of long life." A famous Chinese herbalist who reputedly lived for 256 years—1688-1933—was a devotee of this herb and was wedded to his twenty-fifth wife at the time of his death.

YARROW

This herb was much used by medieval witches. For wedded couples, it was believed to ensure seven years' love.

YEAST

Used medicinally, also believed to possess amorous properties.

YOHIMBINE

This substance, derived from the bark of the yohimbe tree, is native to Central Africa. It is widely used by the Africans for its high sexual potency. It is also known as *quebrachine*, an alkaloid obtained from the bark of the *Quebracho* tree that grows in Chile, Bolivia, and the Argentine. Yohimbine has long been used as an aphrodisiac by the native tribes in South America and in West Africa. Its erotic potency produces its effect on the brain. It also stimulates the nerves of the spinal column which in turn stimulate the genitalia.

ZOLA

Emile Zola, the nineteenth century French novelist, was remarkably sensitive to aromas of various kinds. His fiction is pervaded by this sensibility, particularly in regard to women. In one instance he wrote: "Everything exhaled the odor of woman."

He is responsible, in part, for the reputation of oysters as aphrodisiacs, having written a charming story in which they were featured.

The End